The Young Musician's Survival Guide

The Young Musician's Survival Guide

Tips from Teens and Pros

Second Edition

Amy Nathan

OXFORD
UNIVERSITY PRESS

2008

OXFORD
UNIVERSITY PRESS

Oxford University Press, Inc., publishes works that further
Oxford University's objective of excellence
in research, scholarship, and education.

Oxford   New York
Auckland   Cape Town   Dar es Salaam   Hong Kong   Karachi
Kuala Lumpur   Madrid   Melbourne   Mexico City   Nairobi
New Delhi   Shanghai   Taipei   Toronto

With offices in
Argentina   Austria   Brazil   Chile   Czech Republic   France   Greece
Guatemala   Hungary   Italy   Japan   Poland   Portugal   Singapore
South Korea   Switzerland   Thailand   Turkey   Ukraine   Vietnam

Published by Oxford University Press, Inc.
198 Madison Avenue, New York, New York 10016
www.oup.com

Oxford is a registered trademark of Oxford University Press

Library of Congress Cataloging-in-Publication Data
Nathan, Amy.
The young musician's survival guide : tips from teens and pros /
Amy Nathan.—2nd ed.
    p. cm.
Includes bibliographical references and index.
ISBN 978-0-19-536738-6; 978-0-19-536739-3 (pbk.)
1. Musical instruments—Instruction and study—Juvenile literature.
2. Practicing (Music)—Juvenile literature.   3. Musical instruments—
Purchasing—Juvenile literature.   I. Title.
MT740.N18 2008
784.14'3—dc22   2008021770

9 8 7 6 5 4 3 2 1

Printed in the United States of America
on acid-free paper

One of the advice-giving role models you'll meet in this book is flutist James Galway, shown here rehearsing John Corigliano's *Pied Piper Fantasy* at the Aspen Music Festival in 1985.

Foreword

This is the book I wish I'd had as a kid. Maybe it would have helped me keep on with piano lessons, instead of quitting after nine years of playing when I found myself buried under an ever-increasing mound of homework. If only I had understood back then that playing piano could be a fun, relaxing way to blow off steam, and not just another task on which to be tested, judged, and graded.

It wasn't until many years later, as a grown-up, that I tried music again, with singing lessons. My teacher focused on the joy of music-making, rather than the perfection of the end product, and opened the world of music to me in a way I hadn't experienced as a youngster.

When I had children of my own who showed a flair for music, I searched until I found a piano teacher who could help them discover the joy of playing. They had such a great time that I got up the courage to start piano lessons again with their teacher.

As I observe my slow progress, and the more rapid gains my sons have made, I'm struck by how much fun it is to play an instrument—and how frustrating. Many young musicians keep going despite the obstacles. How do the successful ones overcome the hassles? That's the story this book aims to tell, to aid young people heading off down the exciting, adventurous path of music-making.

For this new, updated edition of *The Young Musician's Survival Guide*, I've rounded up eight additional professional musicians to add their tips to the advice presented by the original edition's team of pros, teens, and teachers. One of the newly featured musicians, Pulitzer Prize-winning composer John Adams, wishes he had known about a few more role models when he was growing up in the 1950s, taking clarinet lessons as a youngster in a small New Hampshire town. Of course, he did have one important role model: Leonard Bernstein, who hosted Young People's Concerts on TV back then. "Bernstein was a kind of movie star to me, who showed that it was OK to be a composer and a classical musician. But today, kids still lack role models in music," laments John Adams. This new edition of *The Young Musician's Survival Guide* tries to fill that gap, jam-packed as it is with fascinating role models: performers, composers, conductors, teachers, as well as talented spare-timers who keep making music even though they've chosen to pursue other careers.

Contents

The Young Musician's Survival Guide

Tune In

1

AMAZING THINGS CAN happen when you play a musical instrument. Magical sounds, marvelous melodies, and razzling-dazzling rhythms can float right out of your instrument—once you get the hang of how to use it. Figuring out how to do that can be fun and also a bit of a challenge. All kinds of hassles can pop up to frustrate even the most dedicated student, such as having no time to practice, getting the jitters before a performance, dealing with pesky fellow musicians, or messing with those big fat music books that flutter shut at all the wrong moments.

If only you could find out from other musicians how they handled these problems.

Now you can! This book gathers together a large ensemble of super musicians to share with you the strategies that have helped them deal with the frustrations they've met along their musical way.

Hot Tips for Cool Sounds

This book's troupe of advisors includes more than 25 professional musicians, interviewed specially for this project. They include quite a few soloists such as violinists Joshua Bell, Hilary Hahn, and Gil Shaham; flutists James Galway, Paula Robison, and Valerie Coleman; pianists André Watts and Wu Han; trumpeter Wynton Marsalis; saxophonists Joshua Redman and Erica vonKleist; and solo percussionist Evelyn Glennie. Also featured are the members of the Eroica Trio and musicians from several major orchestras. Rounding out the roster are composers John Adams and Steven Mackey, as well as conductors Marin Alsop and Gustavo Dudamel.

As kids, these pros often grumbled about practicing and faced the same hassles that bother any beginner. Even today, they can sometimes grow frustrated when working on a new piece and may even have a touch of the jitters before marching out on stage. However, they have found ways to cope and are glad to pass along their advice to you.

"Music is like magic. It can make you laugh, cry, fly."

Also sharing the secrets of their success are more than 150 talented teen musicians. They ranged in age from 16 to 19 years old when they filled out questionnaires for this book, telling how they handled all kinds of practice and performing problems. The questionnaires had been sent to several prestigious music schools around the country, as well as to a few summer music programs and youth orchestras. The teens you'll meet in the book are the ones who volunteered to take time out from their practicing and rehearsing in order to jot down their ideas and suggestions on these forms. (A list of their schools, summer programs, and youth orchestras can be found at the end of this book.) Most of these

young advisors filled out their questionnaires back in the late 1990s when the first edition of the book was being put together. A second group of teens participated more recently, offering input on how music students can make the most of some of the new electronic and Internet resources that have surfaced since this book first appeared. All the quotes from teen musicians in the book come from the comments they wrote down on their questionnaires when they were teenagers. Their tips are practical, creative, and right on target with the kind of advice that music educators give.

Also offering suggestions are more than two dozen music teachers and other musical experts. To pick topics for this huge troupe of advisors to deal with, the author pored over many books and articles on music education, while also sending 200 beginning music students (ages 10 to 14) a "Gripes Form," on which they could list what bugs them about learning to play an instrument.

In addition, the book introduces several spare-time musicians. These are people who still find time to make music even though they are busy with other careers, such as cartoonist Gary Larson or astronaut Ellen Ochoa, deputy director of NASA's Johnson Space Center. She took her flute along with her on one of the flights she made on the Space Shuttle, as you'll see when you turn the page.

Astronaut Ellen Ochoa brought her flute along on her 1993 Space Shuttle mission. Notice the foot loops holding her in place. Without being held down like that, blowing into her flute in the low-gravity environment onboard the Shuttle would have sent her floating around the cabin. Check out the book's Resource Guide for a link to a video clip of another astronaut who loved making music so much that he too took his instrument with him on a mission to the International Space Station.

Magic Time

"You have the opportunity, every time you breathe into your instrument, to make the world a more beautiful place than it was before," notes professional flutist Paula Robison in her *Flute Warmups Book*. Even with instruments you don't breathe into, the same holds true. Basketball star David Robinson made time to tap away at his piano nearly every day while he was playing in the NBA because, as he says, "It gives me joy."

Making music brings joy to our teen advisors, too, who explained on their questionnaires why they're glad they learned to play an instrument:

+ "Music is like magic. It can make you laugh, cry, fly."
  —Janet, piano, flute
+ "I like the energy you feel playing in a group."
  —Justin, sax, guitar
+ "It helps me relax when I'm upset."
  —Frances, sax
+ "I love all the people I've met through music."
  —Jenny, violin, piano
+ "Music lets me express myself in a way words can't."
  —Antony, piano

Singers, Too "I learned piano to help my singing," says Charenée, who also plays flute. Teachers feel it's wise for kids to hold off on taking serious singing lessons until the mid-teen years, after voices have matured. But while waiting to begin voice lessons, future divas can learn a lot about music by joining youth choirs and playing an instrument.

Tune into the Talk

Pretend that all the pros, teens, teachers, spare-timers, and other advisors are gathered in a huge, imaginary practice room. What a crowd! They're waiting to show you that mastering an instrument is well worth the effort. Pull up a seat and listen to these eager-to-help musicians. Tune into their music talk, to help you make the most of tuning into your own instrument.

Spotlight On...

GARY LARSON—Cartoons & Guitar

Food for Thought: "I try to practice guitar every day. If I don't, I feel like I've gone without a meal," says *The Far Side* cartoonist Gary Larson, who started guitar as a kid. "Practicing guitar is a truly enjoyable part of my day, when I can forget everything else and just concentrate on one thing. Even when it's difficult and I feel I've made little headway, I take satisfaction in that I'm still pushing myself. Eventually, I know I'll hear results. It's a little like cartooning. When I started drawing, I could 'see' in my mind what I wanted to draw, but my hand had other ideas. It took drawing a little every day for quite some time before I was able to capture a certain image. But the mistakes I made—the really bad, embarrassing cartoons—were an important part of my discovery process. I try to remember that when I play jazz; when I find myself fighting wrong notes, I recall that this is *supposed* to happen. Playing music is just about the most important thing in the world to me."

Worth It A nationwide Gallup survey in 1994 found that about 62 million Americans play musical instruments; most are glad they do.

Picking and Switching

2

"**C**HOOSE AN INSTRUMENT you'll enjoy or you'll never be motivated to practice," says Ethan, one of the more than 150 older teen musicians who share their experiences in this book. Finding just the right instrument took a bit of searching—and switching—for many of the teens, and for some of our pro advisors as well. How did they hit on the perfect match?

Picky, Picky

Sound snagged many. They heard someone play the instrument and fell in love with the tone. Ethan picked saxophone in fourth grade because, as he recalls, "I heard a tenor saxophone player at the high school who was very good and I knew right away that's what I wanted to play." Like Ethan, many heard a live performance at school, at a concert hall, or at home listening to a friend or relative play. A TV performance hooked Sary, who chose violin after seeing Itzhak Perlman fiddling away on *Sesame Street*. Emily fell for the mellow tone of the French horn when her school's music teacher demonstrated instruments in class. The horn's tone fascinated Adam, too, who notes, "The very first sound I made on this wonderful curly thing sounded like an elephant. I figured any instrument that could do that couldn't be bad."

Spotlight On...

JOSHUA REDMAN— Saxophone

The Right Sound: Jazz star Joshua Redman played several instruments as a kid (recorder, clarinet, piano, guitar, percussion instruments) before zooming in on tenor sax as his main choice. Why did it attract him? "It's hard to explain why you like something," he says. "If someone asks why I like chocolate cake, it's because it tastes good. With tenor sax, I like it because it sounds good. The sound moves me: the warmth and power of the instrument, its incredible poignant character, the sensitivity. I had heard it before I tried it (in fifth grade). It always attracted me. As soon as I picked it up, I felt an immediate connection with it. It just felt right."

Sound wasn't the only attraction. Size drew Lauren to the double bass. "I thought it was amazing that someone could play an instrument that huge," this teen recalls. The trumpet's shiny good looks won over Sarah. Claire chose oboe because "it seemed so exotic." Eric picked percussion after seeing "how much fun percussionists have in a performance."

Chance had a role, too. Often, people played what was available. "I took up flute because we had a flute at home," remembers world-famous flutist James Galway. Another pro, André Watts, settled on piano because as a very little boy "there was a piano in the house and I was allowed to go there and make noise. It felt good. I particularly liked the pedals, holding them down for five minutes and just letting the sound build up."

Some chose an instrument to be like a friend or relative who plays it. Others did the opposite. "My older brother had been taking piano lessons and I wanted to be different," remembers superstar violinist Gil Shaham. When he was seven, his family had two instruments at home: piano and violin. "So it was like, okay, I'll take the other one." Others were steered to an instrument because their school needed someone to play it. That's how Ann Hobson Pilot got started on harp, the first step to her becoming principal harpist of the Boston Symphony. That's also how tuba fever hooked David Bragunier of the National Symphony. "In seventh grade, the music teacher came to my homeroom and said they needed someone to play a sousaphone, the marching-band kind of tuba," he reports. "So the tuba chose *me*. I didn't care. I just wanted to play music. I love an underdog and the tuba is a kind of musical underdog."

Parents also play a role. "My parents decided I should take piano lessons," remembers Rachel Alison. "I loved it so much I kept with it." But love-at-first-playing doesn't happen to everyone, as you'll see in the next section.

Switching

Piano wasn't actually the first instrument André Watts tried. He had taken violin lessons as a very young boy. But when he began messing around on his own with the family piano, he found he liked the piano's "bigger sound" a lot more and switched to piano lessons instead. For professional flutist Paula Robison, the switch went the other way. It was the big sound of the piano that didn't click with her. At age 11, she quit piano when she fell for the flute's high, floating tone.

Some teens switched for other reasons. Randy went from piano to double bass in third grade because he "wanted to play in an ensemble. Piano is more of a solo instrument." He prefers blending into a group rather than being center stage by himself. In middle school, professional jazz musician Erica vonKleist switched to saxophone from flute, which she had been playing since fourth grade. "I wanted to be in the jazz band," she says. "There were flutes in the jazz band, but you couldn't hear them. I thought, 'If I'm going to be in jazz band, I might as well be heard.' The minute I picked up a saxophone, I knew I was meant to play it. I put flute down for a few years but picked it up again in college. Today I do both: classical flute and jazz saxophone."

"Switching is okay, but don't switch too soon. You can't tell about an instrument in just a few months," warns Daniel Katzen, a Boston Symphony French horn player. He started piano at age six and has kept playing it all his life. At age nine he added cello, *not* a big hit. "I never practiced and kept breaking it," he recalls. After two years, he tried French horn. Success, at last! "It felt comfortable right away. I could play it well pretty quickly. I've come to love it."

From then on, he stuck with his horn. "If I had quit again as soon as it got tough, I could have spent my whole life searching for an instrument," he notes. "Other instruments always look cool. But after you start playing, you find that no instrument is really easy if you want to play it well." Give an instrument a good *long* try. You may end up liking it, even though it may be a struggle in the beginning. Remember that just about everyone sounds bad at first.

Is it hard to switch? Yes and no. When Erica vonKleist switched from flute to saxophone, she found that "the fingerings are similar, which helped the transition." But the way of making a sound was different. It took a summer's worth of practice to get the hang of blowing just right into a saxophone mouthpiece to make a good sound. She also had to learn how to take care of the delicate, easy-to-chip bamboo reeds that have to be placed on a sax mouthpiece. "Reeds can be a hassle. I learned to make sure I always have back-up reeds."

If a new instrument wows you, practicing can suddenly become much less of a hassle. Before discovering harp, Ann Hobson Pilot had struggled for years with piano lessons, not liking them and never finding time to practice. "With harp, I felt more expressive. I loved it from the start," she says. "So I practiced more."

Spotlight On...

PAULA ROBISON—
Flute

The Right Switch: "I started on piano when I was about seven, and was a dismal failure," recalls Paula Robison. "It was always a struggle to practice. It just wasn't the right instrument for me. It didn't sing enough. I was a melody woman right from the start. I was always singing." Maybe flute, with its high, singing sound, would be a better choice. A family friend loaned her an old battered flute when Ms. Robison was in seventh grade and gave her a few quick lessons so she'd be ready for group lessons at school. "The minute there was a flute in my hands, it seemed right," she remarks. "It just felt totally natural—like singing. It was like I was made for it. I learned the fingerings in school and copied them down on a little card to take home. I practiced my flute! It was a passion right away."

Adding On

When Lana started French horn so she could join her school's band, did she quit piano? No. She kept up with both. Two out of three of our teen advisors play more than one instrument. So do many pros: Clarinetist Richard Stoltzman also plays sax, pianist Wu Han played viola for many years, trumpeter Wynton Marsalis uses piano for writing music, as does solo percussionist Evelyn Glennie.

"Music is an all-way street. Everything you do in one area helps in another," explains Muh-Huey. This teen's main instrument is piano, but she also plays violin because, as she explains, "It helps me recognize the singing tone in piano pieces." Joel notes another plus to playing several instruments, "It has opened up opportunities to perform in a variety of situations, which I enjoy."

Piano Plus

Many teens began on piano and feel it's a great way to start. "When you're young, immediate results help you stay interested. With piano, you can play basic songs almost right away," says Joel, who began on piano, adding violin later. Knowing your way around a keyboard helps with any instrument. "It's easier to understand scales, half steps, and whole steps if you play piano," explains Cie Ann, who also plays clarinet, violin, and

organ. Abby notes, "If I'm stuck learning something on trombone, I go to the piano and plunk it out so I know what it sounds like." Pro Daniel Katzen adds, "I still visualize the keyboard when playing horn."

Hilary Hahn's main instrument has always been violin, but this professional violinist kept on with piano lessons, too, although she admits, "I never practiced piano much. I didn't like facing the wall on the other side of the piano, sitting in one place for hours a day. But it was a fun instrument to explore and gave me a different feel for music. It has come in handy with reading scores." Knowing how to read piano music makes it easier to read scores for orchestral music, which have multiple staff lines on each page for the different orchestra instruments. As a soloist who performs with many major orchestras, she needs to be able to study the full score before a performance so she knows what all the other musicians on stage with her will be doing during the piece.

Being able to play piano helps conductors, too. "You don't have to be a really accomplished pianist, but you need some piano skills as a conductor to hunt your way through scores," says award-winning conductor Marin Alsop. She started on piano at age two, gave it up to begin violin at age five, but then returned to piano again as a teen. "I wish I'd practiced piano more. I sound like so many people I meet who say, 'I wish I hadn't given up piano.'"

"Don't let anyone stop you from making music."

Go for It

Some kids shy away from a certain instrument because some people call it a "girl's instrument" or "just for boys." Teens who've made bold instrument choices sometimes get hassled, but usually they're not. "As a bass player, I've had to deal with people being sexist toward me. I ignore them. They're either mean or feel threatened," explains Lauren. Abby adds, "I wasn't hassled for playing trombone because I was a *girl*, but because I was so *short* I couldn't reach all the positions on the slide. Don't let anyone stop you from making music." Solo percussionist Evelyn Glennie agrees: "Don't think in terms of 'girl's instrument' and 'boy's instrument.' If there's a chemistry between a person and an instrument, he or she should have a chance to learn it." Katherine, teen trumpeter, notes, "There's no physical reason a girl (or boy) can't handle any instrument. Go for it!"

Spotlight On...

EVELYN GLENNIE— Solo Percussionist

No Limits: "I never thought I wouldn't be able to do this," says Evelyn Glennie of her decision to start percussion at age 12, even though she'd been losing her hearing and was profoundly deaf by then. She was already a very good pianist. "I was curious about the variety of percussion instruments," explains Ms. Glennie, who can sense musical sound through her feet and hands. She was a determined student, and had teachers who helped her become a wonderful percussionist. But when she decided to become a *solo* percussionist and perform by herself (something that almost *nobody* had done), people tried to change her mind. "Those comments fired me up and helped me steam ahead," observes this Scottish musician. She now performs solo all over the world to rave reviews, making music on all sorts of drums, bells, marimbas, and cymbals, as well as piano. "Explore all the ideas you have as musicians," she advises. "Who's to say an individual cannot do something?"

Check 'Em Out

Gary chose his instrument—trombone—to fit into a certain kind of group: a jazz band. Yet Charles picked piano because, as he recalls, "I *didn't* want to be in a band." Not all instruments play in all types of ensembles. This is something to explore before choosing.

Instruments also fill different roles in an ensemble. Some often carry the melody; others tend to have a more supportive role. Allison doesn't mind that her French horn doesn't always get the melody: "I like being in the back-up role, playing harmony. It makes the melody sound better." Other points to consider: Some instruments are harder than others to make a good sound on at first, and some are harder to take care of than others. If you pick one that not many kids play (such as bassoon or oboe), you may be more likely to wind up with a good position in a school ensemble. Your school's music teacher can fill you in on the ups and downs of various instruments.

Cost is something else to think about because some instruments are more expensive than others. Many kids start by renting instruments at school or from a music store, but even the cost of renting quality instruments may be too much for some families. "There are people who can help in situations like that, if a child has a love of music and a willingness to work hard," says Ann Hobson Pilot, who, along with other pros, has been involved in programs for young musicians who need help with low-cost instruments or lessons. To learn of such opportunities, talk with your school's music teacher or with a community music school in your area. (For help in finding a music school, see the Resource Guide at the end of the book.)

Age Game: Pro Joshua Bell (shown at right) started violin at age five. James Galway was nine and Paula Robison eleven when they first tooted flutes. But Ann Hobson Pilot was much older—in high school—when she began harp. Rock guitarist Trey Anastasio of the group Phish was also in high school when he switched from drums to guitar. An early start can be a big plus for learning to play certain instruments, such as the violin, if you aim for a pro career. But with many instruments, getting a later start won't hold you back. If you're dying to begin a new instrument, talk it over with your teacher and give it a try.

The Time Squeeze

3

N O TIME TO practice—that's the number one gripe mentioned by the 200 beginners (ages 10 to 14) who were surveyed about their musical headaches for this book. Finding time is a problem every musician has to deal with, including our troupe of pros and older teen advisors. Not all of them have always been eager to make time for yet another run-through. When trumpet wiz Wynton Marsalis was in elementary school, he definitely had *not* yet become a never-miss-a-day practicer. Flutist Paula Robison remembers in junior high that "there were times I didn't want to practice. When you're that age, there are so many other things you want to do." Even so, she did squeeze in time every day for practice. Before long, young Mr. Marsalis did, too.

Setup Times

Here are three ways our teen experts fit practice into a busy day:

♦ **Same Time:** Many teens practice at the same time each day. It's easier to remember a regular habit. "I tell myself I'll practice clarinet at 7:00 P.M. no matter what. Then I stop everything else and do it," says Stephanie. Meghan's regular trumpet time is just after getting home from school. "Then I have the rest of the evening to do homework, relax, etc.," she says. Maria Beatriz uses a right-after-school time so her piano won't disturb her neighbors. "When I reach the time they don't want me to practice anymore, I do homework," she says. Daniel, however, must have more understanding neighbors. His trombone time? Very early in the morning, before school. Alyssa tackles music "at night after homework is done so I can concentrate on my violin." Michelle notes, "Violin is so soothing after a stressful day."

♦ **Different Times:** Others change their practice slot from day to day, depending on their other activities. Muh-Huey has other reasons for varying her routine. "I usually practice right after school, but if I'm tired and have a lot on my mind and can't put forth my best effort, I do homework first and piano later," she explains. Lauren likes changing her practice time so she doesn't get bored.

♦ **Split Time:** Many teens don't practice in one long session; they split their time into a few short periods spread over the day. Not only can this keep you from getting tired, it also can help those whose minds tend to wander if practicing seems to drag on for too long. "I get frustrated when I practice," notes Cara, a bassist. "By splitting up the time, it clears my head so I can play better." Many teachers agree that several short sessions can work better than a single long one that may leave you bleary eyed and exhausted. Sary uses short violin sessions to take study breaks from homework. For multi-instrument kids, time splitting is a must. "I get up early and practice piano before school," Anne says. "After school, I finish piano, take a break and do bassoon. I play sax whenever I feel like it."

Spotlight On...

JOSHUA BELL — Violin

Fun Time: "There are a lot of hours in the day. I had a lot of interests as a kid. I made time to do things I liked to do," says Joshua Bell, who started violin at age five and soloed with the Philadelphia Orchestra at age 14. "You hear stories about prodigies with pushy parents who don't let them do anything but play violin. That's unhealthy. My parents allowed me to pursue my other interests." He played tennis, then basketball, and next came video games. Now he's into golf. "When I find something I like, I do it a lot," he notes. As a kid, he'd try to sink 20 free throws in a row, or fire away at a video game to be high scorer at the local arcade. "My mother insisted I practice violin every day, even if only for half an hour. Then I could do other things," he reports. "I had plenty of fights about not wanting to practice. I liked practicing much of the time, just not always." In his mid-teens, he went through a phase of sometimes taking off several days. "I goofed off a little too much then. I was able to learn quickly and pull everything together a few days before a lesson. Now, it's harder to learn new pieces than when I was younger. I wish I'd learned more repertoire [pieces] then." But he's glad he did other things, especially sports. "It's good for relieving tension and having fun. It's good to get away from music, get your mind completely off it, so it's more fun to go back."

Working Out

"We musicians train like athletes. When you don't practice for several days, it takes a while to get back to the point you were at before, let alone improve," says Jennifer. As this horn-playing teen has found, playing an instrument is just as physical an activity as playing a sport. The muscles being trained may differ from music to sports. Playing a musical instrument often involves developing fine control over very small muscles such as those in lips or fingers, rather than the bigger muscle groups needed for a bruising tackle or slam dunk. No matter how large or small the muscles, a good way to train them is to give them a regular workout.

Spotlight On...

HILARY HAHN— Violin

Artistic Athlete: "Music can be like sports. That's why you practice every day, for the physical side of things," says Grammy-winning violinist Hilary Hahn. "I've always treated practice like an athletic pursuit. Training technique into my mind and fingers is similar to what an athlete does at the gym. But while polishing my technique, I also practice in order to develop my musical idea of a piece."

A lot goes into her process of deciding how to interpret a piece, from studying the score to listening to recordings. She doesn't try to play differently from other people just for the sake of being different. "If you try to do it totally your own way, it's impossible. The way you interpret a piece is influenced by everything your teachers told you and all the recordings you've heard. If you separate out everything anyone else has ever done, you probably end up with nothing. Well, maybe just some special way of trilling. I might wind up playing a section the way everybody else does, but I make sure I'm not just doing that by default. I need to decide that I really agree with those things and am being true to myself in my interpretations."

She compares this to what she notices in art museums. "When you see paintings of the same subject, a landscape for example, you realize that even though artists use the same materials [paints, brushes, canvas] and paint the same subject, they interpret it differently. My teachers encouraged me to go to museums, to expand my knowledge of expression, to see how an experience is expressed in different ways." She was also encouraged to explore other areas of the arts as a kid: taking dance classes, writing, and creating her own paintings and drawings. "I like how you can express yourself through the arts. It's personal in a way that sports can't be. You can be a beautiful athlete but it's hard to enter an abstract realm of expression on the field."

Every Day... *Really?*

Practicing *every* day is a great idea, but it's not always possible if you're loaded down with school reports or soccer play-offs. Missing a day or two now and then won't ruin your musical future, but our teen advisors try to skip as few days as possible. Half of these 16- to 19-year-olds generally squeeze in some time for their instruments each day. Most of the rest log in five days of music a week.

Some pros were hit-and-miss practicers as little kids. As they got older and more into music, practice gradually became an everyday thing. Now, even though they're famous, they still try to play every day, but may miss a day or two when traveling to concert appearances. As Wynton Marsalis says, "Your playing goes down if you don't practice." The teens agree. Here's what they notice if they skip a few days:

♦ "My fingers feel clumsy at first."
—*Mike, viola*
♦ "My bowing is messy."
—*Joel, violin, piano*
♦ "My lips get a little stiff."
—*Matt, trombone*
♦ "My tone sounds fuzzy."
—*Sarah, flute*
♦ "I mess up runs I've worked on."
—*Kara, flute*
♦ "I'm less coordinated."
—*Will, drums*

Not only muscles grow rusty. Brains do, too. After a few days' break, Alan finds that he forgets "tips learned from my last cello lesson or practice, and my concentration isn't as good."

What about practicing extra long after a few days off? Some teens do that, but overdoing it on your day back may strain the muscles you aim to train. The more often and the more regularly you practice, the faster you'll improve.

"The more you practice, the better you get and the more you'll want to practice."

Jam-packed days are sure to come your way. When they do, try this trick for squeezing in some practice time. "Can you find time to play just one song? Rather than not playing at all if you can't do a full practice, a brief playing will help tone muscles and keep you in touch with what you're learning," observes Vanessa Breault Mulvey, flute teacher at the Longy School in Cambridge, Massachusetts. Gary agrees. On crazy days, this trombonist tries to "practice even just a little, to keep up my 'chops'."*

*Chops? It's not just something to eat. For definitions of musical terms, see the Glossary at the end of the book.

Spotlight On...

WYNTON MARSALIS —Trumpet

Go for the Goal: "Before eighth grade, I didn't want to play music. I wanted to play basketball," says Wynton Marsalis, who first tooted a trumpet at age six. This future Grammy winner took some lessons in elementary school and was in the school band, but he didn't practice much. Instead, he practiced basketball—*all* the time. In eighth grade his game plan shifted. "I started listening to music," he says. "I'd come home from school and put on a John Coltrane record, or a Clifford Brown or Miles Davis. I thought, 'I want to play jazz the way they play.'" One day in gym, it hit him. "I was running up and down, practicing with the team and I said to myself, 'Man, I don't want to do this anymore.' I loved playing ball, but it seemed you could only go to a certain point with it. You could hone your game and beat people, but after that, what? It seemed like music was deeper."

He set a new goal: "To learn how to play music and become better. I stopped shooting a hundred free throws a day and practiced music all the time—an hour in the morning, an hour in the middle of the day, an hour later, or I'd have a rehearsal or gig. I didn't miss a day of practice for seven years." He still had time to hang out with friends and keep up his grades. What about homework? "I did it," he says, "but it didn't take that long. I found if you paid attention in class, you didn't have to spend that much time on homework."

Goal Time

How long should each day's practice session last? That depends on your goals and level of playing. Advanced players generally practice more than beginners, as do those who aim to have a career in music. Among our teen musicians, there's a wide range of practice times. About half of these teens practice from an hour to an hour and a half a day. A quarter of them do more (two hours or more); a quarter do less (half an hour). The average time: a little more than an hour a day.

The pros had a wide range of practice times when they were kids, too. Flutist James Galway was at one end of the time scale. "As a kid, I practiced *all* the time—as soon as I got up, at lunch, as soon as I got home," explains Sir James, who grew up in Northern Ireland and was knighted in 2001 by Queen Elizabeth II of England. "We didn't have TV. I didn't have other hobbies. All I did was play the flute. It intrigued me."

At the other end of the scale was Sara Sant'Ambrogio, the Eroica Trio's award-winning cellist. She started cello at age six and loved it. "But I hated practicing," she says. "I did it every day, but only for 15 minutes." Then at age 14, she went to a summer music camp where they *made* kids practice many hours a day. The staff gave her lots of great music, along with tips on how to spend more than a few minutes practicing it. She loved the challenge and came home determined to try out for a top music school. On her own, she started practicing several hours a day. How come? "I had a goal— a reason to practice," she says. Her practicing paid off—she was accepted at that school.

Several other pros also started slowly as youngsters, gradually increasing their time as their goals became clearer. Jazz star Joshua Redman waited the longest to boost his time—until *after* graduating from Harvard College, where he was one of the top students in his class, earning a degree in sociology. Before then, his main goal was to do well in school; music took a back seat to homework. "In high school, I never thought of having a career in music," he says. "I played saxophone in the band and in jazz combos but didn't practice much." After college, as he was getting ready to go to law school, he realized how much he loved music and knew then that what he really wanted to be was a musician. "Now I am trying to find time to practice regularly," he says.

"There's no substitute for serious practice. If I'd known back then I'd be a musician, I'd have practiced more."

"When I don't want to practice my bassoon, I think of the goal I'm striving for," explains Anne, "whether it's to finish a piece or do a contest. That usually kicks me into gear." There can be short-term goals (learning a tune, preparing for a recital) or long-term goals (trying for all-state groups eventually). Discuss your goals with your teacher to see if you need to add any practice time to help you reach them.

Overtime

Keep in mind that it *is* possible to practice too much. Overdoing it can be rough on tiny, delicate muscles. Also, logging in great amounts of time doesn't guarantee success. "Some of my students come to a lesson and say, 'I practiced so many hours!' And I think, 'So why don't you sound better?' The *way* you practice is as important as the time," says Paula Robison, a flutist who teaches as well as performs. (For practice tips, see Chapters 4 and 5.)

Balancing Time

Do you have to give up all other activities to do music? No! Many teen musicians also participate in sports, student government, debate team, school plays, and all kinds of clubs. "It's hard to fit it all in," admits Jessica, a harpist, who also plays piano while being active on the school paper, ecology club, soccer and track teams. She feels being active helps her music, noting, "If I don't exercise, I don't play music well." Elizabeth adds, "I get antsy practicing cello too long. It's nice to run around playing soccer for a while."

All that running around—or swimming, biking, and dancing—can strengthen the muscles used to play an instrument. For example, aerobic exercise like swimming can increase lung power, making it easier to take the deep breaths needed for wind and brass instruments. Exercise can also relax muscles that may tense up during a practice session.

"It's important to stay in shape no matter what you do," advises Pete, a drummer who loves to ski. Music teachers feel sports and music can mix if you're careful (*ouch*) not to get injured. Many pros were active kids. Joshua Bell played tennis and basketball. Evelyn Glennie swam. Paula Robison took dance. So did Hilary Hahn, who liked to paint, write, and do crafts as a kid, too. "It's good to have lots of interests," she says. "Each day I chose to put time into violin, but it wasn't like that was the only thing I could do and if it didn't work out, I'd fall apart. I knew there were other things I could pursue."

> " ...stay in shape no matter what you do."

Even with the best planning, some teens run out of time and have to drop a few activities. When Keith signed on to play sax in his school's marching band, he could not keep up with other activities because of band rehearsals. But band was so much fun, it was "worth it."

Master Plan

To keep track of her busy life, Patti uses her school planner book to jot down what she has to do and when. "I organize my time so I fit everything in," says this tennis ace who's also into piano, organ, and clarinet. At the start of each week Lauren writes a schedule of when she'll practice double bass. "I stick to it," she claims. Carrie remembers her percussion schedule without writing it. "Just make a plan in your head," she advises. Denise remarks, "Every day is so different. I just try to find time for violin as the day goes by." According to Muh-Huey, a pianist, "It's not a matter of *finding* time, but of *making* time. If you have ingenuity in managing time, there will always be time to practice."

Time-Snatching Tricks

♦ "I do as much homework as I can in free periods at school so I can practice at night."
  — *Randy, double bass*
♦ "I go to the band room during study hall and practice."
  — *Elizabeth Rose, sax, clarinet, piano*

- ♦ "I practice more on weekends."
  — *Emily, French horn*
- ♦ "Watch less TV, or cancel a play date."
  — *David, cello*
- ♦ "The more you practice, the better you get and the more you'll want to practice."
  — *Jenny, violin, piano*

The Home-School Option

In fifth grade, Hilary Hahn switched to home-schooling, partly because she wanted more independence than regular school allowed, and partly because some of her friends had recently started being home-schooled and it seemed like fun. This setup worked well for her, both academically and musically. That's because not long after starting home-schooling, she stopped taking violin lessons in her hometown of Baltimore, where she had been studying violin since she was four years old. Instead, a few times a week, she and her dad made a roughly two-hour drive from Maryland to Pennsylvania so she could continue her training at the Curtis Institute of Music in Philadelphia, a school for mostly college-aged music students focused on performance careers. When she was 12, she also started taking some college classes at Curtis during the week. To make this possible, she and her dad would stay in Philadelphia during the week and drive home on weekends, to see her mom and her Baltimore friends. By then, she had already played her first concert as a soloist with a major orchestra, the Baltimore Symphony Orchestra. Soon she was soloing with other orchestras in Europe and the U.S.

She could, of course, have switched to a regular school in Philadelphia, as some young students at Curtis did. But home-schooling seemed to suit her. "I loved traveling," she says. "I did my homework in the car while my dad drove along." She used special books designed for home-schoolers. "Each year's lessons were right there in the book, with my daily assignments. If I had questions, I could ask my dad."

Your Time

When our teen advisors were younger, several needed an extra nudge to practice. Some earned prizes of stickers and candy, or kept track of practice time on colorful charts. Others had a parent remind them or sit with them during practice. Soon, they stopped doing it for prizes or parents and did it for themselves. "My parents used to nag me to practice oboe. So I didn't want to do it. When they stopped, I got into practicing," says Claire. Jennifer, a horn player, adds, "The desire to practice has to come from inside. You have to want to do it."

Time-Out

What about days when you don't want to practice at all? Maybe school was horrible that day, or it's the first sunny afternoon after a week of rain. "I try to practice flute as often as I can, but if I'm totally not in the mood, I won't practice," says Kim. Nobu-Ann reports, "If I force myself to play when I don't want to, no progress is made. I do something else and come back to the violin later." When the weather is gorgeous and spring fever hits, Stephanie suggests, "I might play my clarinet outside."

"Practicing when you're only half practicing won't accomplish anything. If you can't focus, wait until the next day," says Gary, a trombonist. Natalie agrees, "I try to find a balance between flute and the rest of my life. If I need a day off, I take it." Even pros take breaks. As violinist Joshua Bell notes, "If I've been playing a lot on a big tour and I have a week off, I'll probably take a few days without practicing." He feels that resting when he's exhausted has helped him keep from getting injuries. "But then," he adds, "it takes a little while to get back in shape."

Everybody needs a break. But if you're maxing out on time-outs, maybe the music you're playing is too hard—or too easy. Maybe your music teacher gets on your nerves, or practicing bores you because you don't know what to do. In the next two chapters you'll find help with these and other reasons for taking too many time-outs.

Boring-Practice Blues

4

I F YOU FIND practicing boring at times, you're not alone. Many of our teen advisors feel that way. So do pros. Pianist André Watts recalls, "I liked playing piano as a kid but didn't always like doing the work." As Wynton Marsalis notes in his book, *Marsalis on Music*, "Almost no one likes to practice... You have to spend time working on things that you can't do, which makes you feel bad about yourself. Often it's just terribly boring, the same thing repeated over and over and over again until you get it."

Any activity that involves polishing a skill may get to be dull. Basketball star David Robinson played piano and guitar in his spare time when he was in the NBA. When asked if he found practice boring, he sighed and griped about having to do the same things over and over and over, or, as he phrased it, "The monotony, the tediousness of it." Was he griping about practicing music? No. He meant practicing *basketball* can be boring, along with the training he had to do to stay in shape: running, biking, lap swimming. For him, practicing music was much less of a chore.

"Think of your goals if you're bored," suggests Jennifer, a horn player. "It isn't always fun, but if you don't practice, you'll never be able to play more advanced things. Look at the big picture." Elizabeth does more than adjust her attitude. This cellist found ways to add *fun* to practicing. So did other teens. This chapter is loaded with their boredom-busters.

Top Tunes

So how did Elizabeth beat the practice-time blues? "Besides the cello pieces I'm required to play, I also have a fun piece of my own choice to practice. I do my lesson music and then have fun with my own piece," she explains. Pete, a percussionist, advises, "Take time every day to play stuff you like as well as stuff you need to play." Ben follows that advice. After working on classical oboe numbers, he likes to zip through a few movie themes, or songs from musicals. Stephen relaxes with ragtime after tackling his regular piano pieces.

How can you find sheet music for fun tunes? Brianne uses music she already owns, bringing out some of her old favorite clarinet pieces that she mastered in past years. "I asked my mom to take me to a music store to find books with songs I heard on the radio," explains Frances, a saxophonist. Other sources: Try the library, ask your school's music teacher, or search for sheet music on the Internet. (Chapter 9 has more on using the Internet to liven up practice time.)

Picking Pieces

Renée doesn't just add extra tunes; she makes sure she likes her main pieces, too. "I play pieces I love," this pianist explains. "If I enjoy a song, my playing is better and I have more fun than if I'm playing something I don't like. It ceases to be a chore and becomes an activity to enjoy." Even so, she admits to not wanting to practice sometimes. "I start with a song I *really* like in the hope it will inspire me."

What if you hate a piece your teacher has given you? "When I was younger, I played things I didn't like because they were important to my training," says Jessica, a harpist. "Now I'm at the point where I tell my teacher if I don't like a piece. We agree on pieces together."

Don't dump a piece too soon, warns Joel. "I grow to like most pieces after I learn them," says this violinist. Of course, sometimes you can't ditch a piece, especially if your school ensemble wants to play it. In those cases, Janet, a flutist and pianist, recommends figuring out "what's nice in the piece and learning that first."

When negotiating with your teacher, Austin, a violinist and guitarist, suggests, "Ask for music that motivates you to play at a higher level. It encourages you and makes practicing less boring."

Mix It Up

"I vary what I do. I break up the boring stuff with practicing solos," says Meghan, a trumpeter. Emily not only switches what she does, but where she does it. "Sometimes I take my French horn music outside and sing it to myself," she says. Sary, a violinist, recommends, "Practice in a different room. Do something different and new each time you practice. Variety makes practice time go by fast." That's how David Robinson jazzed up the basketball training he groaned about. Each day he varied his strength-building activities. "That keeps it kind of fun," he observes. "Some people can train the same way every day. I don't happen to be one of them. You have frustrating times in any kind of training. That's what it's all about, overcoming the monotony (the boredom of doing the same thing all the time), while having something inside you that makes you want to do it the best you can."

Spotlight On...

GIL SHAHAM—Violin

Cool Music: "If you're excited about the music, that makes all the difference," says pro violinist Gil Shaham. "As a kid, I found practicing exercises boring, but not the music I really wanted to play. I remember learning the Brahms D minor sonata. I thought it was the coolest piece. (I still do.) Then I walked past one of the practice rooms at music school and heard somebody else play that piece, thinking, 'How can they play that? That's *my* piece!'" That made him realize other kids liked that piece, too. Something else also got him to practice, besides being excited about the music. Every few weeks, he had to perform in front of other kids at the music school he went to on Saturdays. "That gets you to practice," he notes. "You want to get yourself prepared so you don't go up in front of the other kids and embarrass yourself."

Just Imagine

"When practicing, I imagine pictures to go with the music. It makes practicing less boring and helps with the interpretation of the piece," advises Patti, who studies piano, clarinet, and organ. Jeanette, a pianist, notes that "imagining things like a thunderstorm or a figure skater on the ice gets me into the music and its mood." Tiffany, another pianist, agrees: "Get into the sounds of a piece. Some pieces are mysterious. Be mysterious while you play."

Pros use this strategy, too. André Watts explains, "Sometimes I have pictures in my mind when I play. Usually I have feelings, not precise pictures. Possibly I would have thought of a picture as a jumping off point in practicing. I'll remember how I feel when I see that picture. Then that feeling is what I think of when I play. Children should not be embarrassed by the images or silly words they put to music." Not all pros use this technique, but several who were interviewed for this book do. They agree with Mr. Watts that exploring images or stories helps bring music to life.

Move It

Educators have found some kids learn better if they move around rather than sit still when they have to do things like memorize a list of spelling words. With music, movement is a natural. Many music teachers have kids put down their instruments and tap, dance, or act out the rhythms and feelings of a piece. Some music schools let kids explore the link between music and movement in special classes (called eurhythmics or Dalcroze classes).

When an especially difficult violin passage frustrates Michelle, she starts moving about while she plays. "It relieves stress and makes the passage seem a lot more do-able, especially when I play it again later just standing still," she reports. Check with your teacher before trying this, because some kinds of moving around while playing may interfere with good technique. Also, be sure to move carefully so you don't smash your instrument—or yourself. (No cracked fingerboards or chipped teeth, *please!*)

Ann took a workshop given by William Westney, a concert performer and music educator from Texas Tech University who likes to use movement in his teaching. Ann played a piano piece for him. "In one section I was too abrupt," she says. "He had me do a movement exercise with a partner to get a better feel for that passage. I enjoyed it. I have a different attitude toward music now. I try to put more motion into my playing."

Bravo!

"When you practice, picture yourself at a performance, pleasing the crowd," suggests Will, a drummer. That's what Erin does when she practices singing. "I imagine I'm singing for an audience of adoring fans who hang on my every note," she explains. Emily aims high with her daydreams; as she practices French horn, she pretends she's performing with the Boston Pops. Hearing imaginary shouts of "Bravo!" can add spice to any practice session.

Snazzing Up Scales

Now, for the part of practicing many kids long to skip: scales. "Play scales in jazz or funk styles," suggests Justin, who plays sax and guitar. RoseLee, a violinist, snazzes up scales "by playing them in different rhythms, to challenge myself." Nobu-Ann, another violinist, has found that "by adding different tempos and bow strokes to scales, they actually become interesting." Tamara perks up her flute scales by playing them as if they were "beautiful music and really putting myself into them." These are super strategies, according to music teachers.

"I don't view scales as a nuisance. They'll pay off because eventually they'll give me a mastery of the instrument," says Ethan, who's well on his way to mastering sax, piano, and guitar. Pro flutist James

Galway points out, "There are scales all over most pieces you'll play. If you play a Bach sonata or Mozart concerto, you'll find scales in it. They're the bricks and mortar of the house of music." If your fingers can whiz through the scales, you've got a head start on learning lots of pieces—classical, pop, rock, or jazz.

Many pros run through scales every day. Flutist Paula Robison does. So does cellist Sara Sant'Ambrogio, who feels that "playing scales is a great way to warm up your fingers slowly and get intonation (pitch) into your ear." Violinist Adela Peña warms up with "the scales and arpeggios for the keys of a piece I'm about to rehearse, to get my ear going. Some keys are rarely used; so once in a while I throw in a B-flat minor scale, just to make sure I can still do it." Some musicians do scales at the start of practice. Other pros save scales to whiz through as a break later in a session. Flutist James Galway explains, "I still do scales. I might start off on them, but it depends. Sometimes if I get my back against the wall with a difficult piece, I'll start off with that, and do scales later."

Exercise Surprise

Another item that turns up on some kids' least-want-to-practice list is the dreaded technical exercise (also called an "étude," a French word for "study"). Exercises may teach important skills, but their tunes are often less than thrilling. RoseLee perks up violin exercises the same way she does scales, by playing them in different rhythms. Karen, another violinist, suggests whenever possible you and your teacher should try to find études "that are interesting to you, in either melody or rhythm."

However, certain études are important to do, no matter how dull, because they teach skills you really need to master. Even they can be fun, if you attack them right. When Joshua Bell was a kid, his teacher found a way to make his young student actually *enjoy* études. "My teacher didn't like the idea of playing études like a robot," he explains. "He encouraged you to make music even with an étude, to bring out the beauty of it, to make it fun."

Some teachers take a do-it-yourself approach to études. They stay away from traditional exercises and hunt through regular pieces (or pieces a student is working on) to find passages that students can use to practice technical skills they need to master. That's how Sara Sant'Ambrogio mastered the snappy finger work needed for cello.

Spotlight On...

SARA SANT'AMBROGIO— Cello

Her Way: "When I was a kid, I hated études," recalls Sara Sant'Ambrogio, the Eroica Trio's award-winning cellist. "So my dad, who was my teacher, found passages in concertos and other pieces of music that taught the same technical lesson as an étude and I practiced them. It felt like real music. It felt like fun. I'd hear my dad practice the same passage, so I felt like a grown-up." (Her dad was principal cellist of the St. Louis Symphony.) Later when she had to learn the piece that her short practice passages had come from, "I could already play the hard parts of it hands down!" She uses this approach now with her own cello students. So do other teachers.

"I also made up stories for the music as a kid," she says. "When I was eight, I was practicing in the living room and I thought of a movie I saw on TV the night before. I felt like I was playing a sound track for that movie. I got totally into the music. I still make up stories for music I play. I pull events from my own life or make them up. With my students, I ask them about the mood of a piece. We search until we hit on something that happened to them that mirrors the emotion in the piece. I ask them to think about that event and how it made them feel, then play the piece, letting that feeling filter through them. It's so dramatic when this clicks in someone."

Fool Around

Danny keeps his viola and violin sessions lively by "playing music differently than it's written sometimes, improvising on themes, or plucking instead of bowing." Sarah adds fun to flute practicing by "writing my own songs." Benjamin likes to "figure out weird sounds to make with my sax and use them in solos."

Those are great ideas, according to teachers and other experts. "Don't play only what's required for the lesson," says Dr. Eugene Beresin, a psychiatrist for kids at Harvard Medical School who is also a jazz pianist. "I encourage kids to spend time just fooling around with the instrument, getting used to it, making it a part of themselves, so they feel a connection with it."

This helped pro clarinetist Richard Stoltzman when he was in graduate school. At that time, he often got so uptight about playing well that "sometimes I could hardly start playing, I was thinking so hard." A teacher loosened him up by urging him to start a practice session by having fun with the clarinet. Mr. Stoltzman still does this. "Just get up and start doodling around. Don't be too critical of your playing for a few minutes. Be happy. Enjoy the fact that you can wiggle your fingers, take a breath, and out comes this beautiful note."

Dare Ya!

"Play games with yourself. Do something as many times as you can and try to top it each time," suggests Andrea, a flutist. Brianne sets dares for herself on clarinet, such as "trying to hit a note I couldn't hit before." Games helped violin star Joshua Bell stick with practicing when his teen mind started wandering toward visions of video screens. "What kept me going were the challenges," he recalls. "I'd set up challenges for myself, like I wouldn't stop until I did a difficult passage a certain number of times in a row without a mistake. By the time I did it that many times, I'd learned it and made a game out of it."

Besides being fun, this is something many teachers recommend. Often people practice a passage over and over until they get it and then go right on. That means they've played that hard part correctly only *once*, but played it wrong loads of times. Chances are they'll mess up again next time they try it. After you finally do a passage right, repeat it a few times *correctly* to pound it into your fingers and brain.

Play Along

"Just for fun, I put on a CD when I'm practicing and play along with it," says Abby, a trombonist. So does Carrie Lynn, a violinist, who notes, "I find recordings of things I'm learning, usually several recordings of each piece because everyone interprets it differently, and I play along, trying to match the playing." Your music teacher or library may have recordings you could borrow. Courtney, a teen trombonist, surfs the Internet to find recordings of pieces she's learning so she can load them onto her iPod after buying them through iTunes, an online music store. "It's great to play along with the Chicago Symphony or New York Philharmonic. It gives me a better feel for the piece, especially the musicality." Don't get discouraged if you can't keep up with the pros; it's fun to try now and then.

There are also special instructional recordings that give just the orchestral backup for a classical solo, or the background rhythm section for jazz, blues, and rock songs. You play the melody or the solo. Examples of this type of program include the Music Minus One CD series (mainly classical, with some jazz and pop) or the Jamey Abersold Play-a-Long jazz CDs. There's also a software program, SmartMusic, that lets you practice your part while a computer not only plays the back-up accompaniment but also keeps track of how many mistakes you make. "Students can learn their part on their own and see how it fits together with the whole," says Mike Doll, who uses SmartMusic in a middle school in Rock Hill, South Carolina, where he is band director. "Then when we rehearse in class, we can work on balance, blend, phrasing, style, and dynamics, because a lot of the woodshedding [note learning] has been done." (Check out Chapter 9 for more high-tech tips.)

Listen Up

In addition to playing along, it also helps just to listen to recordings—lots of them—and to live concerts, too. Listening time can count as practicing. After all, you're training your ear. "It helps you know what you're aiming for," reports Susan, a cellist. She and our other teen advisors especially like listening to recordings of pieces they're learning. Sarah, a flutist, feels recordings "help you get the mood and expression of a piece." Evan, a pianist adds, "Sometimes I hear a note in a recording that's different from what I've been playing and realize I'm playing it wrong." Listening to a piece can also help with memorizing it and with learning tricky rhythms. Daniel, a horn player, claims to have listened more than a thousand times to John Adams's *Short Ride in a Fast Machine,* partly to master its rapid-fire, repeating rhythms but also because, as he says, "I like the piece. I'm careful not to copy other people exactly but take what I consider to be good ideas and incorporate them into my interpretation."

"Take time every day to play stuff you like as well as stuff you need to play."

Careful listening inspired many pros as kids, and even encouraged Wynton Marsalis to put down a basketball for a trumpet. Joshua Bell got all fired up about working harder on violin as an 11-year-old at music camp where he first heard recordings by violin great Jascha Heifetz. Jazz star Joshua Redman's mom played all kinds of recordings at home—classical, rock, soul, jazz, music from India, rhythm and blues. He soaked it all up. "My teachers have been the musicians I've listened to on records or gone to hear in performance," he observes. "Listen to whatever kind of music you want to play. That music has a language. The way to learn that language is to listen to great examples of it."

A Quick Read

Several teens round out practicing by doing a little sight-reading— playing through a piece cold that they've never seen before. Usually, it's at an easier level than their regular pieces. If you and your teacher pick fun pieces to sight-read, this can not only perk up a practice session but may also help you polish your note-reading skills, and make you braver about tackling new pieces. You'll also be better prepared for the sight-reading part of a competition.

Break Out

"If you start getting bored, take a break," says Matt, who plays trombone. That's what Claire does when playing oboe gets her down. "Do something relaxing and fun for a while and then go back to practicing," she suggests. Experts applaud this strategy, as a way not only to wake up your brain, but also to keep from overdoing it and injuring muscles. (For tips on injury prevention, see Chapter 9.)

Company

Some young kids complain about being lonely when practicing. David felt that way when he started cello. So his father sat with him while he practiced. After a while David got used to working on his cello alone. Shannon often practices flute in school "so I hardly ever find practice boring because I'm with my friends." However, most of our teen advisors prefer practicing alone. Alan explains, "That way I have nobody to impress but myself."

Spotlight On...

ERICA vonKLEIST—
Saxophone & Flute

Listening Up Online: "If you want to play jazz, you have to listen to a lot of jazz music," says jazz saxophonist Erica vonKleist. "There are saxophone players I idolize, but some of my favorite jazz musicians of all time are not saxophone players." As a middle schooler just getting into jazz, she was an active listener, busily trying to learn the tunes and styles she heard on recordings. For example, when listening to Charlie Parker recordings, "I'd learn the melody by ear, then play it on my saxophone, and then transcribe it [write it down on paper]. I'd transcribe his solos, too. If you transcribe something, you'll never forget it. Pick a simple melody to start with and transcribe that. Then get a little more difficult."

During middle school, she did most of her listening and transcribing by putting on CDs. The Internet was just getting started. However, once iTunes came online with its ever-expanding library of albums to sample and maybe buy, she started having fun with a different kind of exploring. "Start with one artist, like saxophone player John Coltrane. Go on iTunes and listen to a bunch of free 30-second samples of John Coltrane tracks and find one you like. Then maybe buy that tune. Then find out who else is playing on that track. Then check them out on iTunes and listen to 30-second samples of their tunes. Find out what they're like. Then check out the people who are on their recordings. You start to learn about this whole circuit of jazz musicians and how they played. It just keeps growing."

Get Into It

"Boring is kind of a catch-all phrase kids use when they don't like something," says Dr. Eugene Beresin, the piano-playing psychiatrist. "Sometimes when kids say practice is boring, they may really mean it's frustrating. They're right. It's very difficult to learn an instrument. You get stuck, make wrong notes and sound terrible. You don't see instant results like with things you learn in school. In school, when you read a new word, you sound it out, learn the meaning, and most of the time you've got it. With music, you play a passage until you get it and then the next time, it's crummy again. It's a different kind of learning than schoolwork."

It's a kind of learning that doesn't come naturally to many peo-

ple. It helps to be taught how to do it—how to become a note detective who can, as Joel describes it, "dissect the hard part of a piece and perfect it." Doing that is a lot more helpful than just playing a piece over and over without much of a plan for how to make it better, as Joel used to do when he was younger. "When I was younger, I wish I'd known how to practice effectively," moans this violinist. "I could have saved myself a lot of time and grief."

The next chapter presents ideas from Joel and our other advisors on how to attack practice time and make the most of it. If you add those ideas to the ones from this chapter on how to add a bit of a bounce to practicing, you'll be in great shape. Practicing is like a complex game that grows more fascinating the more you understand the rules. "Once you know what you're doing, it's not boring," according to Duojia, a pianist. Jonathan, a violinist, agrees, "When I really get into my playing, I don't find practicing boring at all."

Woodshedding Basics

5

"**L**EARNING TO PRACTICE productively is something everybody struggles with," says Evie. This teen cellist admits she used to waste practice time "racing through things" or playing a piece over and over without really thinking about it. Doing the opposite can also be a time waster—playing just *once* each item you're supposed to practice.

It's hard to figure out on your own how to practice well, how to "woodshed," which is musician slang for heavy-duty practicing. Evie turned to her teachers for pointers. That's the way many musicians crack the practice puzzle: A teacher or experienced musician shows them how. Pro clarinetist Richard Stoltzman was in high school when a teacher finally set him on a good practice path. For pianist André Watts, it wasn't until he'd already started his pro career that he found a teacher who taught him to make the most of practice time.

There are lots of ways to practice productively. There's no one "right" way that works for everyone. In this chapter, our advisors tell what works for them. Their tips may help you get more out of practicing, whether you do it in an old woodshed or in your own room.

Warm It Up

"I never practiced seriously until I began the habit of doing warm-ups at the start of practicing," reports Dave. Warm-ups may seem like a needless delay for kids eager to get to the great pieces they love. But as this trumpet player and other teens have discovered, warming up really helps. Slowly waking up playing muscles gets those muscles (and your brain) ready for the challenges a piece has to offer.

Runners wouldn't dream of getting going without stretching and flexing their muscles. Nor would gymnasts, pitchers, ballet dancers, or others who depend on finely tuned muscles to get a job done. Musicians' muscles are no different: They work better, too, if given a chance to get ready. "I always want to go straight to my oboe music, but it's important to do warm-ups," reports Claire. "You'll sound better in the pieces you like to play."

"Warm-ups also get you in the mood," notes Rachel, a teen violinist. Her warm-up consists of practicing scales and an étude or technical exercise. DeDra revs up by working on scales, exercises, and long tones, concentrating on getting a good in-tune sound from her oboe. What goes into a warm-up and how much time it takes differ from musician to musician.

Wynton Marsalis feels a good warm-up needs to cover all the basics involved in playing the instrument. That's how he organized his warm-up when he got serious about trumpet as a teen. "I learned that from basketball," he says. "In basketball, you practice your foot movement, your floor game, going to either side, your jump shot, free-throw shooting.

It seemed like the intelligent thing to do the same with trumpet, to work on all the different aspects of technique."

A teacher can help you pick things to zoom in on for a warm-up. You'll want to include activities that get your fingers moving, as well as ones that let you focus on tone quality and give you a chance to play all kinds of notes: low, high, fast, slow, loud, quiet. You may include scales, or maybe you'll save them for later in your practice session. Solo percussionist Evelyn Glennie notes, "My warm-ups are related to pieces I'm learning. I use passages from the pieces."

"Find a warm-up that makes you happy," recommends flutist Paula Robison, who tries to play hers as musically as possible. "It should be filled with music from the first note, so you warm up that part of your playing, too. If you find a warm-up that's right for you, it can help you get over that dry period when you take the instrument out of the case and may not feel like practicing."

Some musicians change their warm-up from day to day, but Ms. Robison has been doing the same one since she was a teen. "The same arpeggios, long tones, and scales," she notes. "My father used to joke, 'Haven't you learned those things yet?'" Sure, she learned them. That's why she keeps doing them, for the boost they give her. Richard Stoltzman suggests another warm-up tip he gives students. "Don't just put the clarinet together and stick it in your mouth," he explains. "Look at it. Think about the tone you want to make. Hear a tone inside your head. Then play. Get the sound from inside you and then let it come out through the instrument."

Break It Down

After warm-ups, many teens and pros move on to their pieces. They turn thumbs down to just playing a piece over and over without thinking, mistakes and all, hoping that somehow it will improve. "You'll never get anywhere if you keep playing it wrong. The wrong way will get stuck in your mind and be harder to correct," warns Anne, who plays several instruments. Charenée agrees. For her flute and piano numbers, "I play through a piece and note all the trouble spots. Then I work on those." By breaking a piece into bits to work on, "you probably won't work on a whole piece in one day, just one or two sections," warns Claire, an oboist.

Pro violinist Joshua Bell is a break-it-down practicer. "There are times I get stuck technically on a new piece," he explains. "It may have

a fast run that's like saying a tongue twister. For some reason I just can't do it. So I break it into sections. I do just one part of it until I get that right and then add the next part."

"I treat a new piece like a meal," observes solo percussionist Evelyn Glennie. "You don't gobble down all your food at once. You take a little bite, then another, and so on. I learn music in small bites. I take a little part of the music and play it one way. Then I play it another way. I explore different ways of approaching it while not getting bogged down by large bites and getting indigestion."

"A lot of improvement in music is minuscule, tiny little steps forward," notes violinist Hilary Hahn. "Maybe you get better at doing one shift one day and nothing else improves that day. But now you know how to do that particular shift. Next time you practice a similar thing, you'll know how to do it and how to work on getting it better."

Spotlight On...

ANDRÉ WATTS—Piano

Monster Hunting: "I didn't learn to practice effectively until I already had a career," says André Watts, who soloed with the New York Philharmonic at age 16. When he was 19, a new teacher finally taught him how to zoom in on the trouble spots instead of just playing a piece over and over for hours. "If something is wrong in a piece, think about the problem," explains Mr. Watts. "Figure out what's hard about it. If you don't identify what's wrong, it becomes like the monster under the bed. You can't get by him because the guy's always there. He may not come out all the time, but there's always a danger he might come out when you play the piece. You want to get rid of him. Separate that section from the rest of the piece. Mull it over. I might think, 'What kind of motion should I make with my hand to get these notes right? Am I moving too late? Too soon?' Then I go to the keyboard and try it. If it works, I go a little earlier in the piece and pay attention when I get to that spot. Don't tense up. Maybe I'll play the notes that used to be wrong a little louder and unmusical just this one time as I practice, to be sure I get them."

It can take a while to find a solution. "I get frustrated with a new piece. Here I am back to square one, even though I've been playing for so many years! I take a break, come into the kitchen and tell my wife, 'It's killing me! I'm never going to get this.' Then suddenly you wake up one day and you get it! Then you don't even remember how hard it was or why it took so long. While you're struggling, remind yourself that this happens with every piece. You've overcome it before. You'll do it again."

Scope It Out

To deal with the bites that are kind of tough, become a music detective. "I play through a problem area to find exactly what the problem is and what I can do to fix it," reports Ann, a piano student. She gets a kick out of solving these musical mysteries because it makes practicing more of a game. Pete, a percussionist, feels solutions are often easier to find if you "analyze the problem away from the instrument."

It also helps to get some detective training. Like many teachers, Polly Hunsberger gave her students tips for handling trouble spots. "I call new problems 'mud puddles,'" says this professional cellist who taught at Eastman School of Music's Community Education Department. "When you run into a mud puddle, don't go back to the beginning of the piece. Sit in that mud puddle and clean it up. If it's just two notes, play them slowly. Think about exactly where you are, what position. Name the notes and intervals. What's the problem? Is it the rhythm? Intonation (pitch)? The shifting to a new position? The awkwardness of getting there? Think it out. Use your imagination to create a plan to fix it." When you figure out a strategy for fixing the problem, try it. If it doesn't work, try another until the mud's all gone. Education experts say being an active, problem-solving learner like this helps in any subject, not just music.

"I play through a problem area to find exactly what the problem is..."

All that thinking and planning can actually be a big time saver. Pro pianist Wu Han notes, "I used to play a problem passage over and over for hours without thinking." But after she had a baby, suddenly she didn't have as much time to practice anymore. She realized, "I can't waste my time that way. Now I figure out in my mind first what I have to do and then play it. My playing is better!"

Joshua Bell points out that there are "lots of tricks you can use to break up a pattern that gets you confused." Later in this chapter, you'll find a batch of tricks to try. But first, check out the next section, with one of the best tricks of all.

Slow It Down

"At first, I go really slow. It's hard because I want to go fast, but I go slow to make sure I get all the notes right," says Nobu-Ann, a violinist.

"Slow it down until you get control of the notes and rhythm."

Many experts recommend this, both for tackling a new piece and fixing sticky spots in an old one. How slow should you go? "Slow it down until you get control of the notes and rhythm," suggests Adam, a French horn player. Lauren, a double bassist, adds, "It may seem dull when it's less than half speed, but it really does help." Gradually, you will be able to speed it up, after nailing it at a snail's pace.

Lauren and other teens flip on a little machine to aid in the great slow down: a metronome. It clicks away, giving a steady beat, and can be set at different speeds, from super slow to lightning fast. Claire explains how she uses it with her oboe: "Set the metronome way below

André Watts, age 10, at his first performance with the Philadelphia Orchestra in 1957, after winning the orchestra's student competition.

the tempo (speed) of the piece, and practice a passage slowly. Once you can do it at that tempo a few times, increase the metronome speed a couple of notches. Repeat this until you reach the right tempo for the piece." Getting to full speed may take more than one session.

Pianist André Watts uses a metronome for regular practicing as well as for fix-it work. "Don't think of it as someone beating you over the head," he explains. "The aim isn't to play like a metronome. But if you get used to playing with it, then when there's no metronome, you have inside your mind a little tick tock, a little motor you can rely on and that you can put your piece on top of."

"When I was 11, I spent a week during the summer at my violin teacher's house and she taught how to *really* practice. She told me that if you're going to spend several hours of your day practicing, use them so they count," remembers professional violinist Adela Peña. "She taught me to focus on the problems, isolate them, and decide how to solve them. That takes time and a lot of really slow practicing. I still do slow practicing. With the Beethoven Triple Concerto, I take those really crazy fast passages, especially in the last movement, set the metronome really slow, and work it up. I gradually build it up bit by bit, a little faster each time, to where it's flying. Even though I've performed this dozens of times, when I'm redoing it, I always start with slow practicing. It makes it come back so solidly."

Practice Tricks to Try

These practice tips, which help our teen advisors learn a new piece of music or fix a trouble spot, are often recommended by teachers and other music experts:

♦ **"Don't just practice parts you do well. Practice those you have trouble with,"** says Charenée, a singer who plays flute and piano.

♦ **"Make sure there are no distractions,"** suggests Frances, a saxophonist. To help you hear all the cool music you'll be playing, find a place to practice that's fairly quiet.

♦ **"Play a hard passage in different rhythms so your fingers become used to playing it a variety of ways,"** says Alan, a cellist. Claire takes a tricky oboe passage and plays it as if it were written in "triplets or dotted quarter notes or I make up my own rhythm." After a few rounds of this, she tries it again in the correct rhythm. This is one of several ways of changing a passage around to make it easier to learn. How can practicing it *wrong* help you play it *right*? Flute teacher Vanessa Breault

Mulvey explains, "It's a way to make yourself pay attention to the note pattern. It kind of pounds the pattern into your head. You still do the same notes, but by playing them in different rhythms, you challenge yourself to really learn those notes, like a game. It's fun and doesn't seem to make it hard to go back to the correct rhythm later."

♦ **"Play the rhythm on a single note at first,"** suggests Sarah, who does this with trumpet music. This is another change-it-around-to-learn-it strategy. It helps you focus on just one thing, in this case the rhythm, without worrying about the notes. Then try the opposite: Do the correct notes, but play them as whole notes without the rhythm. Then, put both notes and rhythm together. Allison, a flutist, uses another change-it-around practice trick: "I use different articulations (staccato or legato) and then I play it the normal way."

♦ **"Playing a passage backwards helps,"** notes Tamara, who likes to play a run on the flute backwards, and then do it forwards. Or start practicing with the last section of a piece, the one you've probably played less often than the opening measures.

♦ **"Brass and woodwind players can try a hard passage an octave lower,"** suggests Dave, who plays trumpet. After getting comfortable with the low version, he tries it in the higher register.

♦ **"I count the beat slowly, clapping each note,"** points out Justin, who plays sax and guitar. Ann notes, "If I count when I play piano, it really helps."

♦ **"I make up words to go with the rhythm,"** reports Anne, who plays piano, clarinet, sax, and flute. For example, the phrase "ravioli-macaroni pasta" could go with this rhythm:

♦ **"Look for patterns,"** Anne also advises. Does the rhythm in the first measures show up later?

♦ **"I sing a passage before I play it,"** observes James, a trumpeter.

♦ **"Use colored pencils to mark note names or flats and sharps if you keep making the same mistakes,"** recommends Renée, a pianist. Don't be shy about writing on your music if you own it. (If not, make your marks easy to erase.)

♦ **"Fingerings are so important,"** points out Muh-Huey, who plans which fingers to use where in a piano piece so they don't trip over each other. Figuring out fingering helps with other instruments, too. Nathaniel, a bassoonist, notes, "Just because a fingering is in a book, don't assume it's the best one. There are trick fingerings that are useful in certain situations." Ask your teacher.

♦ **"On string instruments, watch your fingers to see where they land, to help make sure every note is in tune,"** suggests Sary. Other string tricks: Pluck the notes; practice just the shifts; "shadow bow" a passage (bowing it in the air); or bow on an open string.

♦ **"On piano, practice hands separately first,"** recommends Rachele. "Leave out some notes in chords," says Andrew, until you get better at a piano piece and can stick back in those notes.

♦ **"I play a hard cello passage on piano to hear what it sounds like,"** reports Wendy.

♦ **"If I try a passage and just can't figure it out, I circle it and ask my teacher,"** notes Kim, who plays flute.

♦ **"Take a break and come back to it later,"** recommends Rachel Alison, who does this when she's struggling with her clarinet. Abby adds, "When I get frustrated with learning a certain passage, instead of throwing my trombone against the wall, I stop and do something else until my temper calms down. I give it another shot later. It's those tricky phrases that turn you into a good musician."

♦ **"Give yourself a reward once you accomplish the goals you set for practicing,"** says Jenny, a violinist. Have a snack, shoot hoops, chat with a friend, whatever.

Hammer It In

"When you get a passage right, play it again instead of just moving on," advises Joshua Bell. That gives you a better chance of getting it right the next day. Let yourself grow used to how nice it feels to do it right. How many times should you repeat it? Experts differ. Pro trumpeter Susan Slaughter of the St. Louis Symphony Orchestra recommends, "Begin at a tempo that allows you to play the passage *perfectly three times*, then *gradually* increase your speed. This method takes patience but it works!"

Spotlight On...

RICHARD STOLTZMAN— Clarinet

Got It: "In high school, I was coming to my lessons not really prepared. I was feeling hassled that I hadn't had enough time to practice," says clarinetist Richard Stoltzman. "I was lucky in having a wonderful teacher then who started me on the road to practicing. Rather than telling me to practice more, he said I probably wasn't using my time well. He had me make a chart outlining what I'd do in every minute of my practice. He had me get a watch with a second hand and time my long tones. They took half a minute each. He said, 'Okay, You'll play three long tones. That's one and a half minutes.' So I'd see they'd take only that long. I timed a scale to see how many minutes it took. I timed everything. I went bananas on the chart. It was huge. I ruled it all out. It had space for 20 years of practicing. I kept the chart for about two weeks. I'd bring it to my lessons. Then one day, he said, 'Never mind. I don't need to see the chart anymore.' I got the point—the chart wasn't the thing. What was important was being aware of what you're doing and what you want to accomplish."

Extra Help—To Go

"I encourage students to record their lessons," says flute teacher Vanessa Breault Mulvey. "There's a lot going on in a lesson and you may miss a point the teacher makes. When you go home and listen to the recording, you'll catch it." Violin teacher Rebecca Henry has found another way to send helpful hints home. During a lesson, she takes a photo on her cell phone and e-mails it to the student's home. This is especially helpful with young kids when she wants parents to understand how to help a child hold the bow correctly. "I'll take a picture on my camera phone and e-mail it to the parent," says this teacher who heads the string department at Peabody Preparatory in Baltimore, Maryland. With older students, if they're standing just right, she'll snap a picture "as a motivation." Some of Ms. Mulvey's students have their own camera phones and she takes pictures with their phones. "It's fun and gives them a point of reference they can look at during the week."

"A great teacher should teach a child how to practice," says flutist Paula Robison. Teachers interviewed for this book agree. "If a child has bad practice habits, I wonder how much the teacher is helping that child with the techniques of practice," says Annette Costanzi, a cello teacher who taught at Peabody Preparatory. She and others take time in a lesson to show a student practice strategies to use at home. Some teachers even give kids a schedule of what to do in each practice session.

Make It Musical

"Knowing the notes isn't enough. A piece must also be beautiful," says Randy, who plays double bass. As Muh-Huey, a pianist, points out, "Part of practicing is trying to convey the different moods, colors, and feelings of the piece." Don't wait until you're note perfect to do this. "Some of practicing is trying to perfect a piece, but some should also be to play through it, faking it in parts if you have to, so you get a sense of it and make music with it somehow," explains Howard Spindler, a piano teacher at the Eastman School of Music.

"You want to say something with the music," observes Boston Symphony horn player Daniel Katzen. "Can you blow the wind in my hair by playing with your imagination? Can you give me a dream in my mind when you play? What's the mood of the notes? Is it a happy note, a mad note, a questioning note?" Study the directions written on the score. Look at the symbols that show dynamics (loud or soft), where the phrases begin and end, which notes to emphasize or repeat. Those directions give clues about the mood of a piece.

"Think of music as talking," suggests André Watts. "If you say something twice, you don't always say it the same. You might say, 'I'm happy. I'm *really* happy.' With music, if a phrase is repeated, play it differently the second time." Mr. Katzen adds, "If you talk in a flat boring tone, no one will listen. There's no way to tell when you're at the end of a sentence. If you put in a comma and pause, and then finish the sentence with an excited exclamation point, people will listen. The same with music." Shape it so it's not just a string of notes.

Reading about composers can help you learn what they had in mind when they wrote music. Some pros also make up stories to get into the mood of a piece. However, Boston Symphony harpist Ann Hobson Pilot uses a different approach: "The audience may see an image, but I just play as musically as I can." To help her do that, she records her practicing. "I can hear if my playing is boring or unmusical, so I know what to change."

"The most important thing when you walk on stage or into the band room is to step up and make your statement," observes pro sax player Joshua Redman. "It's easy to lose sight of that because you're so wrapped up in learning how other people did it. When it's time to play, let the other stuff go. Believe in your own creativity. Give something unique of yourself to the music."

Lighten Up

"Many times I find that a technical problem I'm having on piano comes from tense muscles," says Muh-Huey. "There is such a thing as trying too hard." If that happens to you, lighten up. "Don't be too hard on yourself in practicing," says Rebecca Henry, a violin teacher at Peabody Preparatory. "If you play a note too high, okay. You can fix that, *if* you're calm and your ears are open and you're not beating yourself up for playing it wrong."

Mistakes are bound to happen in practice. "Let them happen, get interested in them, learn from each one. Don't waste time and emotional energy feeling bad about them," advises concert pianist and educator William Westney. He points out that people don't get angry with toddlers who fall while learning to walk. It's expected. The same with music: Expect to mess up while practicing. When you do, think it through. Calmly do your music detective work, and then try again.

Set goals for a practice session. "This way I become focused on what needs to be done," says Muh-Huey. Smart idea, as long as the goals are do-able. "Take one factor at a time." That advice came from legendary violin teacher Dorothy DeLay, who taught at the Juilliard School. More advice from Ms. DeLay: "You might decide to learn just the notes one week. Don't worry about other things, like what your bow is doing, until later. You don't have to learn everything all at once."

Hilary Hahn at age 14.

Spotlight On...

HILARY HAHN—Violin

Colorful Memorizing: "My first violin teacher taught me a good way to memorize pieces," says Hilary Hahn. "The idea is to make each page of the music look different, but do it in a way that reflects the configuration of the music. That gets you thinking about musical structure, which helps keep page after page from seeming like an endless parade of notes."

First, she photocopies the music, so she can try out different ways of marking it up. Then she finds each main section in the music and writes a capital letter at the start of the section: A, B, C, and so on. When a section shows up again in the piece, she marks it with the same letter, but adds an apostrophe to show that it's a repeat. The label A' would note a section's second appearance. If it appears yet again, she marks it A''—adding another apostrophe. She does the same for phrases within a section, labeling them with numbers. She plays through the piece to make sure she has marked it correctly. Then she adds color to the letters. "I make section A red, B orange, C yellow, D green, and so on. I have a photographic memory and can remember how a page looks by the colors. That helps me visualize where I am in the music when playing by memory." If she is sure she has mapped out a piece correctly, she marks up the real score, colors and all. Another trick: "Memorize how each section starts and rattle off the beginnings in order without looking at the music. Sometimes I sing them if I don't have a violin around."

She has memorized hundreds of pieces, but doesn't perform them all each year. However, she keeps her colorful scores to use when she brings back a piece she hasn't done in a while. "I play seven or eight concerti a year, and several sonatas. I try to learn four or five new pieces each season." While learning a new piece, she whips out her markers and uses the same colorful system that has been helping her since she was six years old.

More Memory Tricks

These strategies from the pros can help you drum a piece into your memory:

♦ "Have milestones," suggests pianist Erika Nickrenz. "In a five minute piece, try to have five places where you can start cold. If you get lost in a performance, you can catch the next milestone and go on, instead of having to go back to the beginning."

♦ "I play each hand from memory without the other," adds Ms. Nickrenz. "With piano, there are all sorts of harmonies and chords that you may not focus on as much because you're thinking about the melody. But if you don't commit the accompaniment material really well to memory, that's usually what you lose on stage. I've had a couple of memory slips in performances. I was lucky to be able to continue with one hand. The other hand caught up later."

♦ "I learned a cool trick from a violinist who was in youth orchestra with me," says professional flutist Valerie Coleman. "She said if you can play a piece backwards three times, you've got it. It works! It forces your brain to analyze the piece note by note."

♦ "Repetition helps, letting muscle memory kick in," adds Ms. Coleman. "Play it slowly, then crank up the speed a notch, then one notch more. It's time consuming, but if you memorize a piece this way, you may go away from it for 10 years but you'll still have it under your fingers."

♦ "I graduated from high school with two flute concerti under my belt, the Mozart and the Ibert. I can attribute my learning those concerti to James Galway," Ms. Coleman reports. No, she didn't have a lesson with Mr. Galway. Instead her teacher gave her a CD of the famous Irish flutist playing those pieces. "I listened to that CD so much. Using your ear to learn the notes creates an audio map in your head."

♦ "When I was younger, I made up stories for what I was learning," explains violinist Susie Park. "I would say to myself, 'This is the point in the piece where the girl goes into the woods and sees a woodland elf,' or something like that. That helped not only for memorizing a piece, but for performing it, too."

If You Get Discouraged

"Everyone goes through periods when you get discouraged and don't feel like practicing," points out Tiffany, a piano student. For Gary, this happened right at the start. "My family said I sounded like a dying moose on trombone," he recalls. "But if you just keep trying, you'll get better. You have to crawl before you can walk or run."

Down-in-the-dumps moods can also pop up after you're a good musician. "Sometimes I can't make my flute sound the way I want, or I get frustrated if I don't improve as much as I want," moans Janet. You could be having a bad day, as everybody does. Maybe you have other stuff on your mind, such as school or friends. Or perhaps you've entered a new, harder level and haven't quite mastered it yet. Experts say it's like being a mountain climber who gets stuck on a plateau, a wide flat place. It takes time to scout out a way off that plateau. As Carolyn, an organist, notes, "If you keep working, you'll find a new trail up the mountain." Here's how to get going again:

♦ **Speak up.** "Make sure you tell someone how you're feeling, prefer-ably your teacher," suggests Muh-Huey, a pianist.

♦ **Shake things up.** "Take a fresh look at the music you play," suggests Carolyn. Try to find something new and fascinating about it. If you don't like it or it's too hard, talk with your teacher about playing something else. Joel adds, "When I felt I was making no improvement, I worked on easy violin music for a while to rebuild my confidence." Or shake up your practice routine. "Sometimes I stop practicing pieces to work on getting my tone back," notes Janet.

♦ **Join up.** "I was going to quit trombone. Then I tried playing in the school jazz band and found I liked it. If you get discouraged, try some new type of music, some new type of group," suggests Matt. Piano teacher Howard Spindler adds, "Piano is often a lonely pursuit. So I get my students together all the time. Playing a duet with another kid can help get someone out of a slump. So can being an accompanist for a group at school." The Eroica Trio's pianist, Erika Nickrenz, "discov-ered at age eight how cool it was to play chamber music with other kids at music school. It's like doing a puzzle, being able to pull it together.

If somebody does something unexpected, that doesn't mean it all falls apart if you're listening and play along with their ideas. It's exciting."

♦ **Explore.** "If I get discouraged, I concentrate on another aspect of music, such as I listen to CDs or I compose my own music," says Andrea, a bassoonist. Carrie Lynn, a violinist, suggests another way to explore: "When I struggle with playing the way I want to and wonder why I bother, I improvise. It allows you freedom to express yourself and find points in the music and your playing which excite you."

♦ **Set a goal.** "When I didn't make jazz band my sophomore year, I was so upset I had no desire to play again. But I decided that if jazz band was what I wanted, I'd have to work at it and practice more. Eventually, my work paid off," notes Kim, a flutist.

♦ **Fun stuff.** "When I suffer an overall lack of confidence in my playing, I think about what I really love about music—playing with other people who play well," observes Michael, an oboist. If that's what he loves, he should try to do more of it, suggests cello teacher Annette Costanzi. "Discouraged students should figure out what they like best, whether it's performing, improvising, playing chamber music with friends, or being in a band or orchestra. Do more of that so the most pleasurable thing is what you do most."

♦ **Breathing space.** "I might take a day or so off from piano," says Tiffany. Sary adds, "If you love it, you'll want to go back. After I got away from the violin for a while, practicing became more fun. I practiced more often and improved more quickly."

Makeups

If you can't practice (you've got the flu or are on a trip and can't bring your instrument), here's how to keep up:

♦ "For brass players, buzz your lips or mouthpiece."
  —*Gary, trombone*
♦ "I hold a pencil like a flute and practice fingerings."
  —*Tamara, flute*
♦ "I look over my music and sing it in my head."
  —*Carrie, percussion*
♦ "I listen to a recording of a piece I'm working on."
  —*Randy, double bass*

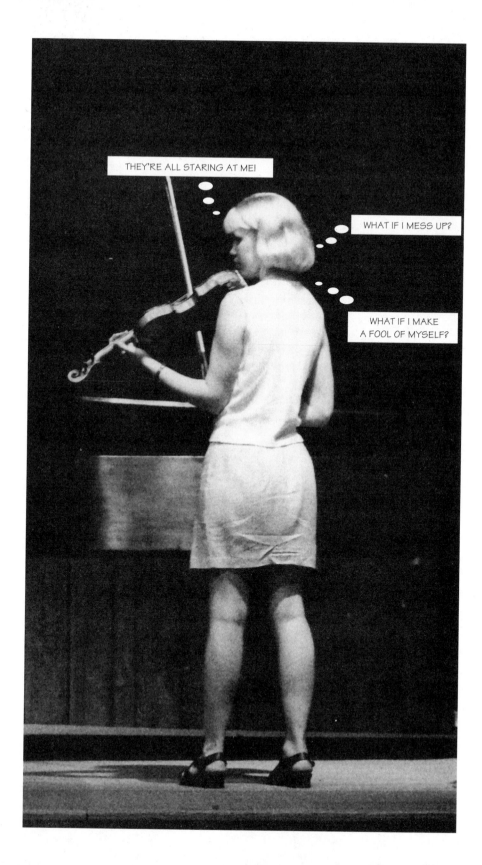

The Jitters

"**Y**OU ALWAYS GET nervous when you perform. That never goes away," explains pro violinist Joshua Bell. "It's just that you learn how to play while you're nervous." He and other pros may look cool and relaxed on stage, but deep inside they've got the jitters, too. As Wynton Marsalis notes, "Yeah, I get nervous. I just try

to look calm and in control when I walk on stage." Those nervous butterflies fluttering in your stomach may not be all bad, according to clarinetist Richard Stoltzman. "I like being nervous before I perform," he
claims. "It makes me feel excited about going on stage and making
music." The trick is to "learn how to deal with the nervousness so it
doesn't get in the way of your playing," explains pro pianist Wu Han.
In this chapter, pros and teens reveal how they do this. By taming her
jitters, Abby, a trombonist, says, "I learned to enjoy my moments in the
spotlight."

Audience Attitudes

"I'm going to let you in on a little secret that can really help you perform," says pro cellist Sara Sant'Ambrogio. "Contrary to popular belief,
most people in the audience are rooting for you to do well. They've
come to have a good time. They may even have paid money to hear you.
They're hoping that you'll play the best you've ever played. They're not
sitting there hoping you mess up. Sometimes kids forget that, because
in music you have to be so critical of yourself. But I've found that most
people come to hear music because they want to have a nice time." Pro
Gil Shaham agrees, "When you play a concert or even just play for
people at home, they want to enjoy it."

Instead of seeing the audience as a pack of snarling beasts eager
to rip you apart, think of them as friendly folks. That helps Abby, who
notes, "I know the audience is there to hear me do well, so I do it." Erin,
a singer, adds, "The audience won't pay much attention to the mistakes.
They want to hear the good parts."

Our teen advisors differ on whether or not to look at the crowd. "I
don't look at the audience. It takes away my concentration," says Sarah,
a horn player. Justin, a sax player, suggests, "Look at some other object,
not at the crowd." For example, you could focus on the back wall of
the hall, so you're looking toward the crowd, without catching anyone's
eye. But Martha disagrees. "I look at them, smile at them, and become
comfortable with them. They make me feel better," claims this singer,
violinist, and pianist. Liza, another singer, finds looking at the audience
helps her feel that "they like you. Think of them as your parents who
hear you all the time."

Of course, there is one kind of audience that isn't so fun-loving: the judges at a competition or audition. But even many of them are probably rooting for you, hoping that you'll play really well and make their day.

Music First

"When you walk on stage, focus not on yourself, but on the music," advises Sara Sant'Ambrogio. On her way onto the stage, this pro cellist thinks, "I hope I'm able to present the music in a way that people can appreciate how incredible the music is, *not* how good I am. That takes the focus off me. Actually, I'm not that important. If it weren't for composers like Bach, when I go out there, I'd have nothing to do. Certainly I'd have nothing as extraordinary to say as Bach does. I've always felt like I'm the luckiest person in the world to be able to share extraordinary music with a bunch of people, so we can experience this together."

" ...it's the music people are there for."

"When you go on stage, remember it's the music people are there for," warns pro Richard Stoltzman. "Sure they want to hear you, but they really want to hear the music. Play it the way you love it." André Watts adds, "Don't think if you'll make a fool of yourself. Think about the piece." Tiffany, a teen pianist, reports, "I let all the energy I have escape into my music and I'm no longer nervous."

How do you keep your mind from wandering off the music? "Concentrate on something in your piece you want to accomplish, such as vibrato, intonation, tone, etc.," recommends Tamara, a flutist. Map out a series of spots in the piece that you want to do in a certain way. Your mind will be so busy thinking about them it'll have no time to worry. "I think about the message I'm trying to get across with the music," reports Rachele, who sings and plays piano. So does Dave, a trumpeter, who points out, "Performing is about communicating to the listener." Pro Gil Shaham notes, "The job of a musician is like being a storyteller."

Get Set

Of course, playing your heart out in front of a crowd is easier if you know the piece really well. "Preparation is the key. To conquer jitters, be fully prepared. I find myself less nervous when I know my piece so well I could play it in my sleep," says Anne, who plays bassoon, sax, and piano. Ricky, a trumpeter, advises, "Practice a piece so much that even if you get the jitters you'll play it well."

Spotlight On...

JAMES GALWAY— Flute

Nail It: "Failing to prepare is like preparing to fail," notes flutist James Galway. He learned to play the flute as a kid in Belfast, Northern Ireland. When he got a chance as a teen to try out for the Royal College of Music in London, he aced the audition and earned a scholarship. The secret to his success? "I learned the audition piece really good," he explains. "That's what you've got to do, really nail it. I practiced all the time. Also, choose a piece in your range—that's part of the strategy." He feels some teachers push kids to tackle pieces that are too hard for them. "I heard a kid play the Mozart flute concerto in a competition recently. She could rattle out the notes, but it had absolutely no feeling. Wait on some of these pieces," he advises. "I learned millions of little pieces before I learned the Mozart concerto."

Trial Run

Practicing a piece for a performance involves more than just getting good at it. You need to practice *performing* it. "I run through the piece without stopping, as if in a concert," says Randy, a double bassist. So does Sarah, a flutist, who adds, "I don't stop, even if I mess up. Afterwards I fix any mistakes I made." Elizabeth, a cellist, recommends, "Play in front of a mirror. Sometimes you'll find yourself making stupid faces when you perform. Not a good thing."

"I run through the piece without stopping, as if in a concert."

Some teachers hold informal practice recitals at which kids play for other kids, to help get ready for the real event. Or you can gather together some friends, your parents, or other relatives and try out your performance piece on them. Pro Joshua Bell uses this strategy. "Just having somebody sit there listening to me play gets me nervous," he reports. "The more experience you get playing while nervous, the better."

"Whenever you perform something, plan to perform it two other times," suggests violinist Hilary Hahn. "No matter how much experience you have, the first time you play a new piece for an audience is nerve-wracking. Part of performing a piece the first time is figuring out how to do it better the next time. But if you don't have a next time and do only first performances, you end up feeling you're always falling short. But in fact, that's not the case. It's just that you haven't figured out yet how to play that piece in public. The more you do a piece, the more different things you can try and see what works. In any individual concert, you don't have as much to lose. You prepare as best you can, of course, but what you learn from the little mess-ups you have in a concert or performing for your family is how to prepare better, how to deliver a better performance the next time."

Record It

Before a performance, some teens record a run-through. "You hear things you're totally unaware of, and then you know what to fix," explains Janet, a flutist and pianist. Jeanette, a pianist, adds, "It helps me learn about things I wish I wouldn't do and also things I like." However, some people hate to hear recordings of themselves or see themselves on videotape. "It's the most uncomfortable thing to hear yourself play on tape," admits pro pianist Wu Han. "It's like hearing yourself talk. But I learned to separate myself from that embarrassment and just judge it as if I were giving myself a lesson. I record myself a lot." (For her recording tips, see Chapter 9.)

Mistake Mania

What if I make a mistake? A worry like that as you step on stage can trip you up. If you're filled with fears about not playing perfectly, that doesn't leave much room in your brain for what it's supposed to focus on: the music. The time to fuss over mistakes is in the weeks of practice leading up to a concert. "I try to remember that my practice has prepared me to play well and I try not to worry," says Joel, a violinist. "If you put pressure on yourself that you have to play perfectly, I guarantee you won't play perfectly," says Jessica, a harp player. Easing up on the gotta-be-perfect pressure makes a musician less tense, which does wonders for improving a performance.

"Even professionals mess up," claims Andrew, a pianist. Is that true? "Yes, of course," says pro flutist Paula Robison. "We aren't machines. Humans make mistakes. If you want a perfect performance, get a synthesizer. Being out there and taking chances—that's what makes playing live music so exciting." Many pros tell the same tale. They prepare thoroughly for a concert and play as well as they can, but they're realistic and know slipups happen. "I make mistakes," says pianist André Watts. "So does everybody. I've never heard of anybody who plays without making a mistake. There are people greater than you who've made more stupid mistakes than you'll ever make."

A performance can still be great even if everything doesn't go exactly as the performer hoped. "You win people over by your tone, by

the quality of the sound, and the message you're trying to communicate," explains Richard Stoltzman. Pro pianist Wu Han points out, "With some mistakes, it's hard for you guys in the audience to tell. I might make a misjudgment in tempo, but I'm experienced enough that I can improvise myself out of it without the audience even noticing."

The same is true for kids. "Chances are nobody will notice if you mess up," observes Stephanie, a clarinetist. Audience members aren't reading along from the score as you play. "Many probably can't even play an instrument," adds Sarah, a flutist. Pro cellist Sara Sant'Ambrogio has even had audience members come up after a performance to say their favorite part was the way she played a certain phrase—the very one she thought she'd ruined!

"Playing an instrument is about making music come alive, not being perfect. Besides, nothing bad will happen if a note slips," says Tiffany, who plays piano. Stephen, another pianist, agrees, "I don't think about not messing up, but about playing musically. I go out there and do my best, knowing I might mess up a note or two. But if I feel I've gotten a musical message across to the audience, then I played perfectly."

Spotlight On . . .

GIL SHAHAM — Violin

Jitters Tamer: "As a little kid, I didn't have jitters. Later on, I went through a period of getting really nervous before performing, almost like I was paralyzed," recalls Gil Shaham, who started violin at age seven in Israel, and continued studying in New York after his family moved there. He soloed with the New York Philharmonic at age 12, and the London Symphony at 17.

When he got older and went through his stage fright period, he says, "I went out and played because I had to, but I didn't enjoy playing so much. Then I sat myself down and said, 'This is ridiculous! I can't get so nervous every time. Who cares if you have a memory slip and forget the rest of the piece? What's the worst that can happen? It's not like I'm a heart surgeon and someone will die.' That solved it for me, realizing the amount of nerves I had was related to taking myself too seriously. I realized you can get things totally out of perspective. Some passage that a violinist is worried about doesn't matter at all for the audience. They just want to enjoy it. Now, when I go on stage, I'm prepared to make a fool of myself. Now there's no problem. I love playing."

Applause, Applause: "Everybody makes mistakes in performance," according to violin teacher Dorothy DeLay. "It's not anything to worry about. What you want to do after a concert is see if you can trace down what happened so you can fix it. But don't do that the day of the concert—maybe two weeks later. You want to feel when you've finished a performance that you've done something good. And you have! Probably most of the notes were fine and the audience had a good time." Rebecca Henry, another violin teacher, adds, "Usually kids complain about things they didn't like in a performance, but it's important for them to say what they did well, too."

Rescue Mission

If you make a mistake, here are some tips on how to keep the performance from being a total train wreck:

♦ **No faces.** "The worst thing is to make a face," cautions pro harpist Ann Hobson Pilot. "That lets the audience know. Don't let on that it happened and don't let it rattle you."

♦ **Forget the flub.** "That mistake is over, it's gone, it's yesterday, even though it was just a second ago," advises Sara Sant' Ambrogio. Randy, a bassist, warns, "If you dwell on a mistake, that leads to more problems." Lana, a horn player, adds, "I tell myself it was no big deal. If I'm really into a piece, I'm too busy feeling it to think about mistakes."

♦ **Don't stop.** "I keep playing to give the illusion that my flub was on purpose," says Josh, a trombonist. If you're totally lost, "stop only for a few notes or beats, take a deep breath and pick up again. I never repeat anything," advises DeDra, who plays oboe. Alyssa, a violinist, adds, "Pretend it's a rest. Often, the audience doesn't know your piece."

♦ **Make it up.** "If you can, improvise for a moment until you find a place to continue," suggests Jessica, a harpist. Paula Robison adds, "Sometimes it's fun to see how you can work your way out of a mistake. That's why it's so important to learn to improvise."

♦ **Think forward.** "Never think backwards. You always have to be in the moment and focusing forward on what's coming up next," advises Ms. Sant'Ambrogio. As Elizabeth, a cellist, points out, "The most important note is the next one." Katherine, a trumpeter, suggests, "Get excited about how well you're going to play the rest of the piece. Give it your all."

Flub-Free CDs: If everyone makes mistakes, how come you don't hear mistakes on CDs? Recording engineers use tricks to fix the bloopers. An engineer can have a musician record a messed-up passage again until it's right. The error-free version is inserted into the recording in such a way that listeners will never know.

Spotlight On...

ERIKA NICKRENZ—Piano

Shoes and Rulers: "I practice in my concert shoes," says Erika Nickrenz, the Eroica Trio's pianist. "If you wear flats when you practice but three-inch heels when you perform, your legs will be at a different level." That changes how it feels to use a piano's pedals. "I try to get the rehearsal environment as close as I can to the performance environment. I even try to get the rehearsal room lighting really bright, as it will be on stage. It feels different playing in bright lights." She also knows how many inches below a keyboard she likes a piano bench to be. She brings a ruler to concerts, goes on stage before a show, makes some measurements, and fixes the bench height.

These are some of the strategies she has come up with over the years, ever since playing her first big concert, at age 11, as the soloist in a Mozart piano concerto with her music school's orchestra. She didn't have much time to learn the piece. "I was filling in for an older kid who dropped out a few months before." Besides practicing her part a lot, she hit on another idea: "I went through the piece in my head a lot. At night in bed, I'd 'play' every note in my head. That helped me memorize it really solidly." Also helpful, of course, was having a few rehearsals with the orchestra. So was the run-through she had with just one other musician, a pianist who played the "piano reduction"—a special version of the concerto in which all the notes the different sections of the orchestra play are rewritten in such a way that a single pianist can play them. This kind of a run-through helps a soloist grow comfortable with how her part fits in with what the orchestra will do. "I had some butterflies waiting backstage before the concert, but I was prepared. You're less nervous if you're well prepared. I had a great time. I got a taste of what it was like to be a professional. It whet my appetite for more."

Mind Games

"So much of music is mental, like in sports," observes Joshua Bell, who shoots baskets and putts golf balls in addition to fiddling his Stradivarius. "With basketball, you imagine (or visualize) the ball leaving your hand and going into the net. With the violin, you kind of visualize the sound by hearing it before you make it and then imitating the sound you have in your head. With a difficult shift, it helps if you imagine what it's going to be like if you hit it right. It's all about confidence. In sports, if you lose your confidence, your game goes to pot. The same with music." Several teens use visualization, too. Carrie, a percussionist, explains, "Imagine yourself playing your music perfectly." This not only helps in performances, but when you're practicing, too.

"If you think you can't, you can't. It goes the other way, too."

Another mind-calmer is to admit you've got the jitters (like everyone else), and then, instead of freaking out, shift your attention. "Distract your mind," advises Carrie. Meghan, a trumpeter, thinks of "a calm place." Michael, an oboist, says, "I imagine I'm practicing at home." Amy, who plays sax, notes, "I tune out everything around me."

Some teens do physical things to distract jittery minds, such as stretching, doing jumping jacks, relaxing their muscles, buzzing their lips, or wiping their hands and sprinkling on powder to keep them from getting slippery. Ann, a pianist, notes, "My hands shake before I play, but if I shake them even more, they stop!" Frances, who plays sax, adds, "Sometimes a good laugh helps." Daniel, a trombonist, uses "deep breathing" to calm down.

Do a "worst case/best case" analysis. What's the worst that can happen if you play badly? What's best that can happen if you do well? Chances are you won't get whisked off to do a solo at Carnegie Hall if you're great—nor will your friends abandon you if you miss a note. Emily, a horn player, reminds herself, "It's not the end of the world if a mistake is made." When Elizabeth Rose plays piano, sax, or clarinet for an audience, she keeps in mind that "there will always be another performance, so relax."

If all else fails, fake it. "The moment I walk on stage I look absolutely confident because that's what I want to be even though I'm actually nervous," says Jessica, a harpist. As Sydney, a pianist and singer, notes, "Attitude is 98 percent of the game. If you think you can't, you can't. It goes the other way, too."

"When you get up on stage, if you keep in mind that you're giving a gift to the audience, that your performing comes from a place of love, that can help make the nervousness go away," says flutist Valerie Coleman. "Music is a gift that we can give to make others feel good, to inspire them."

Pep Talk

Before marching on stage, André Watts gives himself a pep talk. "I always get nervous," he admits. "So I say to myself, 'Look, André, you played this piece great last month. You've been working. There's no reason there should be a problem. Don't get silly now.'" Teens use pep talks, too. Here's what they tell themselves:

- "After all your hard work, you deserve to play well."
  —*Duojia, piano*
- "Hey, I'm not going to let my nerves ruin my efforts!"
  —*Muh-Huey, piano, violin*
- "I've done it once—I can do it again."
  —*Ben, oboe*
- "Enjoy it. This is my time to shine."
  —*Andrea, bassoon*
- "The technique is there. Trust it."
  —*Adam, French horn*
- "I keep thinking positive, that I'm just going to make music and have fun."
  —*Maria Beatriz, piano*
- "This performance will be only thirty minutes of your life."
  —*Caedmon, singer, flute*
- "I know this music. I can do it. Go for it!"
  —*Wendy, cello*

Pre-Concert Routine

"Check out the concert hall," advises pro James Galway. "Check out the lighting, the acoustics. The sound of a hall can affect your playing. You need to know what you're up against. You'd hate to be suprised." This is especially important for pianists. Wu Han notes, "I try the piano in the hall before I play, but usually you don't have time to have it tuned the way you like. You learn how to adjust and not be bothered too much."

Paula Robison tries out the hall not only to learn how her flute sounds there, but because she feels "in every hall there are the vibrations of everyone who has played there before. Concert halls are filled with a kind of energy. If you open yourself up to that, it can be vitalizing for a player."

Pros also check out themselves before a concert. "I like to take a nap in the afternoon before a concert," says Joshua Bell. "It gets me relaxed and fresh. I practice slowly and try to keep calm. Usually I don't play basketball before a concert." Solo percussionist Evelyn Glennie adds, "I don't like to be too busy on a concert day. It should be an easy day so I have time to rehearse, get to know the hall, eat something, have fun, and joke around."

Of course, you also need to check out your instrument to make sure it's ready to be played. Look it over a few days before a performance so you still have time to rush to a store to get any supplies you need—reeds, strings, valve oil, cork grease, rosin, and so on.

As for last-minute warm-ups right before the performance, there's a difference of opinion among our teen musicians about whether to play the piece that will be performed. Some like to play through the piece or certain sections of it. Others prefer to save the piece for the show so it's fresh. They warm up instead doing scales or other kinds of exercises.

It Gets Easier

"It takes time to get over the jitters. The more you perform, you'll notice them going away," says Matt, a trombonist. So if you aim to conquer the jitters, scout out ways to do more performing. Some possibilities: Join an extra ensemble in school or at a community music school, play for visiting relatives, form a pick-up group with friends, play at churches or other houses of worship. Wu Han found another way to increase her on-stage time as a kid in Taiwan. "When performers came to my school," she recalls, "I'd sign up to turn pages for them so I could get on stage and see how it's done."

"I was scared the first few times I had to improvise, playing my own solos in middle-school jazz band," says saxophonist Erica vonKleist. "I was a pretty quiet kid, didn't speak up much in class. In fact, people would kind of talk over me in class. But when I improvised, that meant everyone *had* to listen to what I was playing. I kind of dug that. I got over that initial scared feeling." It also helped that once a week high school kids came to her school to show the younger kids how to improvise. "You get used to doing it and realize you can make up melodies, check out the harmonies, use different kinds of chords. It all just snowballs."

Spotlight On...

WU HAN—Piano

Do It: "I used to do a whole routine before a concert: I had a hot bath in the afternoon, I took a nap, and had a nice dinner," remembers Wu Han, who grew up in Taiwan, attending a high-powered music school there before coming to the United States in her late teens. But after she and her husband, David Finckel (cellist with the Emerson String Quartet), had a baby, there wasn't time any more for a relaxing pre-concert bath, nap, and dinner. "After my daughter was born, I didn't have time to fool around and pamper myself. I'd take her with me to concerts. When the orchestra managers knocked on my dressing-room door before a concert, they were shocked to see me in my jeans playing on the floor with my kid. I'd think about the piece when taking care of her. A few minutes before the performance, I'd get dressed, put on my makeup, and go on stage. It's fantastic. I play so much better now! I think the bath and that routine made the performance seem like a big deal. Now I have limited time. When I go on stage it's like, 'Great! Let's do it. I have my chance.'"

Not Always First: Even pros missed getting top parts as kids. "I wasn't always first chair in band in high school," says Richard Stoltzman. "I'd freeze up in tryouts. I didn't mind playing for audiences, but I didn't like to play for judges, to prove how good I was. I just liked to make music."

Spotlight On...

SUSIE PARK—Violin

The Real Reward: "I started doing little local competitions in Australia when I was five," says Susie Park. "My success at these early competitions was a result of not even being aware that I was competing. I thought I was just playing a concert!" As she grew older and entered bigger competitions, including ones in other countries, she began to realize that these events were indeed contests, ones she wasn't always going to win. "I was much more aware that there were a lot of other talented violinists out there. That added an extra challenge to the mix." She remembers at one international competition she entered at age 13, "I got into the semifinals but not into the finals. It was a tough lesson to learn, that things weren't always going to go the way I wanted. It wasn't always smooth sailing."

Luckily, she developed a way to cope with these high-pressure events, which she kept entering because she felt they were good performance opportunities. "My mom told me it's not about winning. The prize isn't why I play music. I play because I love music and want to share with the audience what I want to communicate about the music. I tried to remember what had been different when I was really young and competing. I realized that I played better when I just tried to enjoy it. When I felt like I had a mission, a goal to tell people a story through the music or show them what I was feeling inside, that really helped me. I started learning that it's not about the end result. The real prize is knowing I gave the best performance I could." Having this new attitude improved her performances. "If I had only a greed to succeed, that wasn't going to produce a good performance. It would be full of that kind of feeling. But if I was giving something of myself, expressing something, that was more fulfilling for me and for the audience."

Competition Savvy

Competitions can cause jumbo jitters. These events are a big part of music for many students, who are often encouraged to enter music contests by their teachers.

Some of the main competitions for kids are run by music teacher organizations at the state or local level. In these events, a student spends months preparing a piece, often one from an approved list. At the competition, judges hear the student play the piece, and may also ask the student to do some scales and sight-reading. Students who receive the highest scores are often invited to perform in an all-county or all-state ensemble.

In some competitions, participants may just receive a score sheet on which a judge comments on their playing. In others, winners get to play in a special recital. At more advanced levels, there may even be a money prize. Other types of competitions involve trying out for a place in a local youth orchestra, or at a conservatory. To learn what kinds of competitions are available for someone at your level, ask your music teacher and talk with older music students at your school.

"Some kids like competitions, but others can't stand the atmosphere of them," says Paula Robison. She liked competing as a kid, unlike Gil Shaham and Richard Stoltzman, who hated playing for judges.

Our teen advisors note that competitions have both good and bad points. "They're an exciting challenge and give you something to work for," observes Caedmon, a singer and flutist. Gary, a trombonist, adds, "It's good to work hard on your tryout piece. The process is often worth more than the results." But Sarah, a trumpeter, gripes, "It's a lot of pressure." Kristen, a singer, agrees: "Some competitions put too much pressure on kids to be the best rather than simply to enjoy performing."

"Competitions often come down to luck—how you feel on a certain day or what mood the judges are in. Talented people often get turned away," warns Tammy, a flutist. Denise, a violinist, adds, "Don't let competitions become too big a part of your playing." Janet, who has played in many piano competitions, concludes, "They're fun, but only do them for the performance opportunity. Always remember: The best don't necessarily win. People who don't win are sometimes just as good."

Competition Calm

To control competition jitters, try the strategies already covered in this chapter, plus these extras, suggested by the pros:

♦ **Start early.** "I always prepared way early for a competition. That's the way to beat it," says Wu Han, who won many piano competitions when growing up in Taiwan.

♦ **Do it all.** "Really know your stuff," advises Paula Robison, who aced her share of auditions. "Know your part. Know your scales. If you'll have to do sight-reading, practice sight-reading."

♦ **Rest.** "Don't stay up all night before the audition worrying about it," Ms. Robison adds. "Get enough rest."

♦ **Keep to yourself.** "At the audition, don't be distracted by other players," Ms. Robison warns. "Don't listen to them and worry that they play better. Say to yourself, 'I'm the one who's playing, who has something unique to give the judges. I'm going to do my best.'"

♦ **Forget the prize.** "Don't think about the possible consequences of playing well or not playing well," warns Joshua Redman, who got jitters under control at the Thelonious Monk Institute of Jazz competition in 1991 (which he won). "If you worry too much about the consequences, you won't be able to get in touch with that part of yourself you need to reach to create. Put your faith in the moment."

Wait: For kids who feel way too nervous to perform, skipping the upcoming concert may pay off in the long run. That's what Nathan did when he was a little guy in his first year of piano lessons. Instead of doing the recital that terrified him, he played his pieces privately for his grandpa. A year later, a more confident Nathan took part in his teacher's spring recital.

The Peer Scene

7

MAKING GREAT
NEW friends
is one of the
best parts of
playing an instrument. But, as with
any activity, you're bound to run into
a few kids who get on your nerves.
Our teen advisors have met their
share of pesky players, such as the
know-it-alls who boast about their
so-called skills while dumping on
other people's playing. Also annoying

are chatterboxes who talk through rehearsals, blasters who play too loud, stand hogs who set up a shared stand so only they can see the music, and jabbers who poke you with their bows (or flutes or trombone slides). Here's how our experts survive.

Deaf to Disses

"Mostly, I ignore critical kids. They stop when they see you don't react," advises Allison, a horn player. Matthew, a double bass player, agrees, "Ignore them. Think about your part."

Pros use the same tactics. "When I was a kid, other kids tried to bother me and sometimes really got me down," remembers cellist Sara Sant'Ambrogio. "I just tried to focus on the music. I also kept a little bit off to myself so I wouldn't get sucked into any of that." Pro hornist Daniel Katzen advises, "Learn to cut away from those that detract from you and make friends with people who treat you well."

Sometimes, it's hard to keep calm. One way to do so is to figure out why the know-it-alls do what they do. Maybe they're trying to be helpful. Maybe you *are* too loud or out of tune. If so, fix it. But if the criticism seems mean and not helpful, "they may have little self-confidence," notes Sarah, a horn player. A truly confident player doesn't need to boast. Another possibility: "The other person may be jealous of your success," points out Andrea, a sax player.

Wynton Marsalis recalls, "I ran into that all the time as a kid, people putting you down, that whole petty nature of the 'in' people. It was harsh, but it made me happy. Remember, I played ball. I knew when your opponent tries to destroy you verbally, that's a sign you're beating him. It didn't make any difference whether they put me down. I was going to practice. There was no way it was going to rattle me." Tammy, a flutist, adds, "Take comfort in the fact that you won't have to play with the same people forever."

Other disses to ignore come from kids who don't even play instruments. "I try not to let it bother me. It's a shame

Wynton Marsalis at age 16

those kids can't appreciate music. But they have their things they like to do, and I have my thing I *love* to do: music," observes DeDra, an oboist. Anne, a bassoonist, notes, "The older you get the less of this you encounter." Many teens never run into it at all. As Pete, a percussionist, notes, "Everybody knows the really cool cats are in the music department."

Speak Up

In some situations, it helps to speak up *politely*. "During performances, my stand partner would talk to me," says Stephanie, a flutist. "So I'd whisper, 'I'll talk to you later.'" End of problem. Courtenay, a singer, stopped chatterboxes at chorus by "calmly and politely telling them I need to concentrate so could they please leave me alone."

"There's no room for attitude when you're playing with others."

"If someone kept pointing out when I messed up, I'd say in a nice way, 'Could you please stop because you're making me nervous,'" Stephanie recalls. Ben, an oboist, advises, "Say to them that you know you made a mistake and are trying to fix it."

Speaking up can actually help the critics, too. "I used to laugh when somebody messed up," one teen admits. "I didn't realize it could hurt people until someone told me what I was doing. I don't do that anymore."

Joe, a drummer, suggests a different strategy. "If I don't agree with the criticism, I say, 'I'll ask the instructor,'" he explains. That's what many teachers recommend. "We prefer that band members not correct each other. If you're annoyed with a player, tell the instructor," advises Ken Peck, who taught music in a Westerville, Ohio, high school. "If a kid bugs another kid, we deal with it on an individual basis. Of course, if someone isn't sure of a fingering, we encourage kids to give that kind of help. If a person plays a wrong note, a reminder that 'Hey, it's a flat,' is okay. What we don't like are negative comments."

Try to solve a brewing conflict before you explode. One teen remembers growing more and more angry in rehearsals with a fellow player's out-of-tune playing. Finally, on the day before the concert, the annoyed teen blew up. Later she realized it would have been better to have said something earlier, either to the out-of-tune player or to the conductor.

Work It Out

Often simple common sense can come to the rescue. "When a jabber is near, I sit a little father away than normal," says Nobu-Ann, a violinist. RoseLee, another violinist, recalls, "Once I sat next to a girl who shoved her bow into my knee every time she made a down bow. I finally told her to sit up straight. The problem went away."

To avoid stand-sharing problems, Allison, a French horn player, tries to get her own stand, whenever possible. "Or compromise with your stand partner," she suggests, "such as alternating who'll turn the page." David, a cellist, observes, "Page turning is done by the person in the inside seat." Amy, a saxophonist, advises, "I always make sure the stand is in the middle between us. If I'm told to turn the page because I'm in a lower chair, I swallow my pride and do it. It's not worth getting all worked up."

Spotlight On...

SUSAN SLAUGHTER—Trumpet

Team Spirit: When Susan Slaughter became principal trumpet with the St. Louis Symphony Orchestra back in the 1960s, she had trouble with another trumpeter. "He was an older player. I could see him bristle whenever I said something to him," she recalls. "I took him aside and asked if we could clear the air. He said he wasn't used to taking orders from a woman and needed time to adjust. I realized it was his problem and he had to work it out. It took about two years, but it has worked out fine." As principal, she's in charge of deciding which member of the trumpet section plays which solos. She has tried to build team spirit within the section. "With my assistant, I try to give him things to play that are challenging. I might take things away from myself that I'd like to play and give them to him. For the rest of the section, when they do well, I tell them. I try to give the spotlight to others when it's appropriate rather than grab it all for myself."

Humor Helps

What about narrow-minded sexist comments that might be aimed at some kids for their instrument choice? "Humor is a good way to handle these things," notes Barbara Butler, trumpet professor at Northwestern University. Ms. Butler started trumpet in fourth grade at a time when not many girls played the instrument. "I got some grief from other kids for playing trumpet, but from my viewpoint it was a challenge to show them I can do it," she recalls. "I never saw it as negative until I got older. Then it seemed really unfair that anything like that could get in the way of your progress." Sexist remarks occasionally popped up in college and when she started playing in orchestras. After trying a variety of tactics, Ms. Butler settled on humor. "If there's a group mentality where people start to pick on somebody, if you can flip back with humor, it defuses the situation. People start thinking your reply was pretty funny. That puts the teasers in their place. If they can't get under your skin, they'll turn their attention elsewhere." What if you're short on jokes? She advises, "Just say, 'Hey, that's enough of that.' Don't get all hot and bothered."

Susan Slaughter, principal trumpeter of the St. Louis Symphony, recalls, "There were comments made when I was in school, but I'd laugh them off." She has run into some sticky situations in her career, but usually a calm approach has smoothed things out. If that doesn't work, she suggests talking with the officials in charge.

Jealous?

Maybe the reason why a fellow player ticks you off is because *you're* jealous. That can really mess you up, according to Patti. "For a while,

I didn't have any fun playing piano because I was trying to be as good as or better than this person who also took lessons from my teacher," she explains. "Erase those feelings! You are your own person. You have your own talents that make you an individual. Don't let jealousy make you less of a performer."

"Don't let jealousy make you less of a performer."

"It's okay to be a little jealous if it makes you work harder. But too much jealousy makes you feel bad. I play cello for fun. Don't make it a contest," warns Elizabeth. Rachel, a violinist, suggests, "Stop comparing yourself with that other person and start comparing your playing with how you were before."

Good advice, according to pro cellist Sara Sant'Ambrogio, who learned to control pangs of jealousy as a kid, thanks to her dad. She recalls, "My dad used to say, 'You're not really competing with anyone except yourself.' You're competing to control your *own* performance, to play as well as you can, which doesn't have anything to do with how the other person sounds. It's not like there's just one pie of talent, so if someone has a larger slice, you'll have a smaller slice. Talent is infinite. Like love. There's room for everyone. Everyone has unique gifts. I don't allow myself to compare myself to others. I try to recognize the gifts others have and also the gift I have. It's your responsibility to bring as much joy as you can with that gift." As Carrie, a percussionist, notes, "There will always be people greater than you." Don't go bonkers every time you run across one of them.

Losing Out

For kids in ensembles, jealousy may bubble up if you don't get picked for the part or solo you feel you deserve. Our teen advisors know all about that. "At first, I was bitter and depressed and immature about the whole thing," says Michael, remembering a time he missed out on getting a special oboe part in orchestra. "Then I decided I'd just have to play better." Joel, a violinist, adds, "Sometimes I've wished I got a higher part, but realized eventually that I really was where I belonged."

"I try to make the part I got sound extremely musical and well played," recalls Elizabeth Rose, a clarinetist and sax player. Karen, a violinist, suggests, "If you play the part you got as best as you can, maybe the conductor will notice and switch you into a better part later." Actually, your part may not be so bad after all. Elizabeth, a cellist, points out, "Often it's harder to play the second chair part than first chair." Adam, a horn player, adds, "If nobody played the second or third parts, there'd be no harmony!"

In jazz big bands, the solos often go to the player of the second part. In some youth orchestras (and in some professional ones as well), players may trade off who plays the first chair part in different pieces. Janet, a flutist, once even suggested to her conductor that he have "a rotating schedule of who gets to be section leader." Or a conductor may ask an excellent musician to play the third chair part to keep the group's tone well rounded. If only weak players do the lower parts, the ensemble may end up sounding mighty sad.

"Conductors in school and youth orchestras often choose soloists by age rather than by ability. Eventually, you'll be the oldest, too," advises Tammy, a flutist. When you do get to the top of the heap, Carrie Lynn suggests remembering how you used to feel. This violinist had always been irritated that only the first chair player in her orchestra played solos. "When I got to be first chair, I arranged with the conductor for everyone to have a chance to audition for solos," she says. "If they can beat me, they deserve the solo."

If you're very unhappy with your placement, a calm chat with the conductor or teacher may help. You can learn what you need to work on to land a better spot.

Spotlight On...

EROICA TRIO—

Getting Along: "When we rehearse, we have fun, but the goal is always to make the music as good as we can," says violinist Susie Park, the newest member of the Eroica Trio. She joined the trio in 2006, right before its twentieth anniversary. The group's original violinist decided to take a break from being in an ensemble that spends so much time on the road giving concerts. Ms. Park's violin teacher at the Curtis Institute recommended her to the trio's pianist and cellist. They invited her to read through some music with them, as a kind of audition. After the first few minutes of playing together, all three realized they were meant to be a trio.

"We've been having the best time together," says Erika Nickrenz, the trio's pianist. "Before the first rehearsal of a piece, we each prepare our individual parts so we can play through them with few mistakes. We each form an idea of what we'd like to do with the piece, but not so rigid that we're not willing to change it. Then we come to rehearsal, start playing and listening. We feel our way through the piece and adjust as we go. I might hear that one section is going in a different direction than I had imagined. When we finish playing a section, we talk about it. You can't say, 'I want to do it this way because it sounds pretty.' You have to have reasoning behind it. If we have different ideas, we'll try it each way and then come to a decision. If two of us really like a certain way, the other goes along. Sometimes we find later that an idea may not work well in a performance. Then we'll go back in rehearsal and re-work it. Even with a piece we play a lot, we still rehearse it. We review how it's gone in past concerts, what's worked and what hasn't."

School Music Blues

As kids become better musicians, sometimes the school orchestra and band may not seem so exciting. The music may be too easy. Other students may goof off too much. As one teen gripes, "It bothers me when the other people drop their bows and instruments and laugh about it." Another complains, "It's frustrating when people don't care enough to play what's written but just hit any note they can." Here's what our resourceful teens do:

♦ **Brainstorm.** "Go to the teacher," suggests Lauren, a double bassist. Together you may turn up ways to make your school experience more challenging. "When you have kids at an advanced level in a large ensemble and have lower-level students as well, it is important to pick music that is challenging, but not ridiculous, or you will kill the ensemble. The lower-level students will never be successful," explains high school music teacher Haig Shahverdian of West Hartford, Connecticut. He challenges his better players by letting them also play in small ensembles, having them write music, and urging them to try out for non-school groups.

♦ **Low-pressure zone.** "I enjoy orchestra class in school for what it is: a time to play fairly easy music with other kids," says Joel, a violinist who also joined out-of-school music groups.

♦ **Make the most of it.** "The great thing about music is there's always more to learn, no matter what your level," says Josh, a trombonist. Sarah, a flutist, points out, "Easier songs provide opportunities to work on tone, intonation, and dynamics." Cello teacher Polly Hunsberger encouraged all her students to play in their school groups, even kids good enough to win places in youth orchestras: "Sharing your accomplishments with your peers is important. So is being able to help others. Besides, rehearsals are an ideal time to review basics. Think about how you could play the notes in different positions, with different fingerings. Practice your vibrato. Always play your best."

♦ **Leadership time.** "Sometimes you have to be the leader for others to look up to. Remember how you enjoy playing with musicians of higher caliber. That's how kids in school feel about playing with you. Be *flattered*, not annoyed," suggests Elizabeth, a cellist. Randy, a bass-ist, adds, "Never feel you're doing the ensemble a favor. The key to success is team spirit. Being independent kills it. Do your best."

Spotlight On...

GUSTAVO DUDAMEL— Conducting & Violin

Youth Orchestra Wiz: At age four, Gustavo Dudamel conducted his first orchestra— made up of little toy soldiers. He imagined that his toys were playing music he heard on recordings or at performances of an orchestra in which his father played trombone. "There was always music in my home," says Maestro Dudamel, who grew up in Venezuela. He pretended his toys were in famous orchestras, such as the Berlin or Vienna Phil-harmonic. Years later, when he actually conducted those orchestras, he joked that "I've conducted those orchestras before."

He made the move from pretend conducting to the real thing, thanks to youth orchestras. Venezuela has more than 200 youth orchestras that provide free music lessons in an effort to spark an interest in music among youngsters from poor neighbor-hoods, such as the one where he grew up. The hope is that the self-confidence, discipline, and teamwork skills that come from orchestral playing will help young people no matter what careers they follow as adults.

Maestro Dudamel was 10 when he began playing violin in one of these youth orchestras. "At age 12, my teacher put a baton in my hand and asked me to conduct part of a rehearsal. From then on, it was conducting all the way!" He kept on with violin, but also studied conducting. "Playing an instrument and understanding what a player goes through can help a conductor. I learned my friends in the orchestra want to express themselves and make music as much as I do." The more chances he had to conduct his fellow youth orchestra members, the better he grew at encouraging and inspiring them. He became so skilled that by age 17 he was the official music director of the top ensemble: the Simón Bolívar Youth Orchestra. When it toured to other countries, the infectious enthusiasm of this young conductor won rave reviews. Major orchestras invited him to be a guest conductor. Then came an amazing honor—being named, at age 26, music director of the Los Angeles Philharmonic. "I love living with music," he says, adding that "I still practice violin and love to play."

Gustavo Dudamel celebrating with members of the Simón Bolívar Youth Orchestra after a concert.

Branch Out

Another way to solve the school-music blues is to join ensembles outside of school. "In advanced ensembles there won't be so many students with pesky problems. Playing in a great-sounding group and being surrounded by players at your own skill level (or above) is exciting," explains Tammy, a flutist. Carrie Lynn agrees, "You have a chance to play with people who share your enthusiasm for music."

Escaping pesky schoolmates isn't the only reason to join these ensembles. Pete, a percussionist, reports, "Being in a youth orchestra turned me into a real musician." Tamara, a flutist, adds, "It's also a lot of fun, which is the most important thing."

Most of our teen experts joined groups outside of school, such as youth orchestras, or community orchestras and bands that are made up of teens and adults. Many of these teens also tried out for (and got into) all-county or all-state ensembles. Others joined special ensembles at school or at nearby music schools, or formed their own groups, playing not only in youth orchestras, but also in rock bands, jazz combos, and pit orchestras for school musicals.

These musical extras rate high with our teen experts. "In youth orchestra, we play much more challenging music than at school," reports Jenny, a violinist. Carrie Lynn adds, "In groups outside of school, you're exposed to players of a higher caliber, which makes you rise to their level, or get closer to it. This helps keep you humble. Getting a big head definitely doesn't help your musical growth."

Summers are also music-filled, with summer camp programs or workshops at music schools. Summer programs can let you really zoom ahead. Josh, a trombonist, notes, "Playing all day for weeks on end increased my playing level. It's possible to learn great amounts in less time in a camp atmosphere." Malena, a horn player, points out that music camp "keeps chops in shape over the summer." That can help you avoid the oops-it's-September-and-I-haven't-played-a-note-all-summer nightmare. Many pros did extras as kids, including Wynton Marsalis. In high school, he went to music camps, formed a funk band with his brother, and played in all-state and community orchestras.

Ensemble Etiquette

Musician-to-musician squabbles can pop up in any ensemble, no matter what kind. To cut down on this bickering, it helps to follow the rules of ensemble etiquette. "When I was in high school, my teacher told me the secrets of professional etiquette, like not to be a wise guy," says Todd Seeber, who plays double bass with the Boston Symphony. He discovered that in professional orchestras there's a chain of command that helps keep things running smoothly.

Each section in the orchestra has a leader, its "principal" or "first chair" player. Players in a section are supposed to discuss problems with the section leader, who then may discuss them with the conductor. Often school and youth orchestras use a similar system. Here are other basics of good ensemble manners:

♦ **Don't stare.** "Don't stare if someone plays a wrong note. It can happen to anybody," warns Todd Seeber, double bassist with the Boston Symphony. As David Bragunier, who played tuba with the National Symphony, points out, "If somebody clams a note and you jerk your head and stare, that lets the audience know."

♦ **Fit in.** "Play with the section," Mr. Seeber advises. If you disagree with how it's playing, don't just do your own thing. Talk with the section leader. If that doesn't help, speak with the conductor (or instructor) during a break.

♦ **Be a team player.** "Ensemble playing is a team effort," he adds. "Advice and directions traditionally come from the conductor or section leader. So telling your stand partner what to do can be seen as poor ensemble manners. Work things out diplomatically and constructively."

♦ **Write neatly.** "Don't scribble all over the score," he also suggests. "Write notes neatly, and not in pen." That way when you hand the music back, your notes can be erased. Chances are other players will have to use the same sheet of music in future years.

Spotlight On...

STEVEN MACKEY—
Composing & Guitar

Rock Out: "I never took electric guitar lessons," says Steven Mackey, a composition professor at Princeton University. He never learned to read music until he was in college. Yet from ages 10 to 19, he became awesome at electric guitar, teaching himself by messing around with the guitar and amplifier set his parents bought him. "I was playing totally by ear, listening to records, or hanging around older kids who knew more about guitar than I did and having them show me things."

As a teen, he played in rock bands with friends—garage bands that actually practiced in his garage. "I started making up my own songs. That's the wonderful thing about the garage-band world. There's no distinction between playing and composing. If there's a place in a song for a guitar solo, you have to think up something. I didn't write down my songs. I'd memorize them and teach them to the band. I was interested solely in rock music then. I'd never heard any other kind."

When he finally discovered classical music (which he heard for the first time in a college music-appreciation class), he was blown away by the power of such composers as Beethoven and Stravinsky. He was also intrigued by the fact that they wrote "music that's intended to distill all of life into a listening experience rather than being music to dance to or do laundry by. I decided that's what I want to do." He switched his major from physics to music and now writes award-winning orchestral and chamber music that often has a whiff of rock and roll to it—and sometimes even an electric guitar solo. "If I could do it over, I'd probably learn to read music earlier, but in a way it was a fine way to do things. I developed a positive attitude about composing and a feeling that music is something fun to do with other people. We'd practice in my garage and rock out. I still have that feeling when I compose, in my basement now, rather than in a garage."

Teamwork

"People may get on my nerves, but I don't like to cause trouble about it because that leads to problems within the ensemble. Teamwork is necessary in ensemble playing," explains Sarah, who plays flute. Elizabeth, a cellist, adds, "There's no room for attitude when you're playing with others."

Jazz pro Joshua Redman observes, "What you're trying to do is come together with other musicians to make a statement. If you're just out to serve your own interests, you might as well play by yourself. In an ensemble, you're trying to create something greater than yourself. To do that, everyone has to treat everyone else with respect and sensitivity. Every musician has to think: 'How can I use my individual talents to serve the interests of the group?'"

"We call ourselves a family and we want to keep it a happy family," explains high school music teacher Ken Peck. "If there's a problem in the band, we sit down with the individuals involved and iron it out." What if the problem involves a teacher or conductor? Take a look at the next chapter for helpful teacher (and conductor) tips.

Teacher Talk

8

A NDREA'S SAXOPHONE TEACHER "inspired" her to become a more expressive performer. "He helped me find the passion within myself to play, and showed me how to express that in the music. I didn't know I could do that," she says. "His encouragement brought me to places I never thought possible." But sometimes things don't go so well between student and teacher, or between student and conductor. Our troupe of teens and pros talk about what makes a good teacher, how to find one, how to get along with both teachers and conductors, and helpful strategies to use when things aren't quite working out.

Good News

"You need somebody to have faith in you, to make you believe you can do something fantastic," remarks pro pianist Wu Han. She was only lukewarm about piano during her first years of taking lessons. Then, at age 13 something changed. She got a new teacher who turned her on to piano. "Before, I never had much confidence. This new teacher thought I was talented and put a lot of energy into teaching me. I worked very hard for her."

That's part of what makes a good teacher—someone who knows how to encourage you to do your best. Of course, it's also essential for a teacher to be well trained, both in music and in teaching kids. Here's what some of our teen advisors have liked about their favorite teachers:

- ◆ "He took his time, didn't rush me, and helped me work through my problems."
  —Daniel, trombone
- ◆ "She understands that no one is perfect."
  —Kara, flute
- ◆ "He was fun and made music fun."
  —Abby, trombone
- ◆ "She gave praise, but not too often to spoil me."
  —Alan, cello
- ◆ "Good teachers understand a student's personal style and are willing to work with that rather than forcing the student to conform to the teacher's style."
  —Tammy, flute, piano
- ◆ "They broaden your horizons and teach about music in general, not just the notes."
  —Stephanie, clarinet
- ◆ "If you make suggestions, they take you seriously."
  —Elizabeth, violin

Students play a role in making the relationship with a teacher work, according to Paula Robison. "Keep yourselves open to the ideas of a good teacher," she advises. "When you go to a lesson and the teacher suggests playing it a certain way, really try and do it. You might like it. Later you can go your own way when you're by yourself."

Group-Lesson Option

Our troupe of teens and pros have taken both group lessons as well as private lessons. They report advantages and drawbacks to each.

Many teens started learning to play their instruments in elementary or middle school, learning the basics from the school's music teacher in a class with other kids. Many pros started that way, too, including Paula Robison, Richard Stoltzman, and Joshua Redman.

Group lessons at regular school have several advantages, besides being free. "You don't lose your confidence because everyone else is just as frustrated as you," explains Andrea, who started sax that way. Sarah, a flutist, notes, "It gets you used to playing in front of others." Malena, a horn player, adds, "It's fun and there's not much pressure." Many schools have excellent teachers who are skilled at many instruments. However, a disadvantage of group lessons is you may not progress as fast as in a one-on-one situation.

Several teens started with another type of group lesson, by enrolling as very young kids in a Suzuki class at a community music school or conservatory. Learning with a group is a big part of the teaching method developed more than 60 years ago by Japanese educator Dr. Shinichi Suzuki. Also important in the Suzuki method is having a parent learn to play the instrument with the student and take notes during a lesson so the student knows what to practice.

Susie Park, the Eroica Trio's violinist, was three years old when she started learning violin with a Suzuki teacher. "My mother started learning violin with me for a short time," says Ms. Park, who grew up in Australia. Her mom hadn't played violin before, although she had sung in a choir when she used to live in Korea. "My mother was extremely important in my early training. She would motivate me. I loved violin, but she made it really fun. She created a scrapbook. Each page was for a piece I was learning. She drew cool designs on each page. One was of a big turtle with a shell made up of lots of little sections. Every time I practiced the piece, I colored in a section of the shell. I loved coloring and was excited to finish the drawing and see that, wow, I had practiced the piece 200 times!"

Her mother also sang the Suzuki tunes with Susie as they walked down the street or went on trips. Suzuki students start learning pieces by ear, just by hearing them. The more Susie hummed those tunes, the better. By age six, she had learned to read music and switched to a teacher who didn't use the Suzuki method. Her mom had stopped playing violin, but still tried to help her musical daughter. "My parents always had music playing in the house. That developed my ear even more." Having a good ear has been useful in memorizing new pieces. "Listening to recordings of a piece helps me learn it."

Spotlight On ...

RICHARD STOLTZMAN—Clarinet

Don't Stop: "I was lucky all the time in having great teachers," says Richard Stoltzman, who started studying clarinet with group lessons in fourth grade at elementary school. "It wasn't very inspiring music, but what was inspiring was the teacher. He was enthusiastic and cheerful, no matter what." In junior high, the school band director told the boy's father that his son had real talent and needed a private teacher. Richard had actually first gotten interested in clarinet because his dad, who worked for a railroad, played clarinet and sax in his spare time. "It took a while to convince my father to pay somebody to give me lessons. He felt I was doing it just for fun." Finally, they found a private teacher at the local music store who taught him classical and jazz tunes.

Then, bad news: The Stoltzman family had to move to a new city. "I was so sad to leave that teacher. At my last lesson, he looked me in the eye and said something like, 'You can do it. You can play music. Don't stop.' If somebody believes in you, that makes you say to yourself, 'Well, this person believes in me. So even if I don't think I can do it, I guess somehow I better keep doing it.'" At his new school, the band director found Richard Stoltzman a new private teacher who also believed he could do it. And he did.

Private Lessons

After mastering the basics in group lessons, many teens and pros found a teacher to give them private, one-on-one instruction. Some did this after a few months of group lessons; others waited until after a few years of group classes. Once they found a private teacher, many teens still kept on with their group classes at school.

However, a few never switched to a private teacher. Jazz star Joshua Redman never had a private teacher, even in high school, but took lessons at regular school.

Malena feels private lessons helped her a lot. "Private lessons help with every aspect of playing, from the technical to learning solos," she claims, having found at age 14 a private horn teacher, after three years of group lessons. Personal attention from a teacher who's an expert on an instrument can make a big difference. "You can learn at your own pace," adds Jessica, a harpist.

Some teens take private lessons at their regular schools, studying one-on-one with the school's music teacher, either during or after school. Others study with private teachers outside of regular school. There are all kinds of private teachers, such as independent music teachers who give lessons at home, teachers associated with a music school or conservatory, as well as teachers who give lessons at a music store.

Pros like Joshua Bell and James Galway went through a series of teachers as kids. Both started with a friendly neighbor who may not have been the world's best musician but who knew how to get a kid excited about music. Later, each moved on to more advanced teachers at a music school.

A big drawback to private teachers is the cost. One-on-one lessons are more expensive than learning with a group. But there are ways to make private lessons more affordable. Read on for money-saving ideas.

Money Help: To help with the cost of private lessons, many music schools have scholarships or lower fees if families have trouble affording lessons. To learn about such opportunities in your area, talk with the music teacher at your regular school or contact the National Guild of Community Schools of the Arts to learn of music schools that offer scholarships. (See the Resource Guide at the back of this book.) Another possibility is to be tutored by an excellent high school musician. Several of our teen advisors give lessons to younger kids, charging less than professional teachers. Contact the music departments at local high schools. One high school teacher has even set up an after-school program at elementary schools where his better teen musicians tutor younger kids for free. However, it's very important for a teen tutor to have a professional teacher to turn to for guidance.

Spotlight On...

BARBARA BUTLER—
Trumpet

Tough Stuff: Barbara Butler started trumpet in fourth grade. "I got private lessons in school from the band teacher," remembers Ms. Butler, a trumpet professor at Northwestern University. In seventh grade she met the teacher who really turned her on to music. "He was a college professor from my town. I took private lessons with him all through high school. He had me do stuff that was way over my head. That made it seem like a challenge. He wanted me to become a better trumpet player and didn't care what people thought you should do. He didn't make me work on scales (which I, of course, needed to do and had to catch up with later). He just kept giving me some of the best music ever written for trumpet. He never told me a piece was hard. He said it was a great piece and to do it for the next week. He gave me fun things like Al Hirt solos or he'd say, 'Here's a piece they're doing at the conservatory in Paris.' I was getting busy with other stuff like ballet and track. If he just gave me exercises, I'd have gotten bored and quit. I didn't play the pieces perfectly, but he kept me totally interested."

The Search

If you decide to find a private teacher, a good place to start searching is with the music teachers at your regular school. They may give private lessons themselves, as is true of Lana's band director, who was her first private horn teacher. They also usually know of good teachers in the area. "We asked several public school music teachers for recommendations of trombone teachers and one name kept popping up," recalls Gary. Other places to try: music stores or community music schools that offer after-school and weekend classes.

You could also call a local orchestra or the music department of a nearby college or university. That's where Wynton Marsalis found teachers as a teen growing up in Louisiana. "I had a lot of teachers," he explains. "I would seek people out because I wanted to learn how to play. I used my teachers as a resource." Some taught at colleges; one was in the New Orleans Symphony. They taught him different skills. One showed him how to play the piccolo trumpet; another worked with him on orchestral playing.

Getting to Know You

Once you get the names of a few private teachers, check them out. Learn what training and experience they've had. Talk with some of their students. If possible, you and a parent should observe a lesson or have a trial lesson. Discuss your goals with the teacher. Find out what the teacher expects in terms of practicing, lesson time, and recitals. Some teachers have all this information written in an agreement they expect students to sign.

A good teacher won't mind this checking. "I'd never start teaching anyone who hadn't come to observe a lesson first," says cello teacher Annette Costanzi. "They may know of my reputation, but how do they really feel around me? It's not like school where you have no choice. You have a choice! It's good to want to get to know the teacher first." The more you know about the teacher and what's expected, the less likely there will be problems later.

Still Learning: Even after becoming professionals, many musicians continue to use teachers. Joshua Bell would check in from time to time with the teacher who had guided him as a teen. Richard Stoltzman would sometimes visit the teacher he had at Yale, or would try things out on a friend who runs a clarinet choir. "We musicians can be pretty critical of ourselves, but sometimes we need that outside ear of a teacher listening," he says. Wynton Marsalis uses a different type of coach. "Sometimes I get students I know at the Juilliard School to critique my playing," he says. "They hear things I can't. That helps when I'm getting ready for an album."

Stormy Weather

Most of our teen and pro advisors have liked their music teachers, both those at regular school as well as private teachers. But a few teens grumble a bit. Some gripe about teachers who are "overly critical." Others groan about those who give too *much* praise. Also annoying to some teens are teachers who talk too much, don't explain things, or can't keep the rest of the class under control. Here are strategies the teens have used when they've had hassles with teachers both in regular school and in private lessons:

♦ **Deal with it.** "I learned not to take the teacher's criticisms so personally. I realized the teacher wasn't criticizing to be mean, but to make us better," explains Emily, who plays horn. Allison, another horn player, notes, "Some teachers yell because they care."

♦ **Talk.** "When I feel I'm not going anywhere in my lessons, most times a conversation with the teacher clears things up," says Rachel Alison, who plays clarinet and piano. Sometimes students get grumpy if they don't like the music a teacher selects. "I talk with my teacher about it and we compromise," explains Andrea, a bassoonist.

♦ **Parent support.** "Have your parents talk with the teacher," suggests Ben, an oboist. This is especially useful if the difficulties involve the style of teaching. A chat with the counselor may also help clear things up if you have difficulties with a teacher at your regular school.

Spotlight On...

VALERIE COLEMAN— Flute & Composing

March On: "I was in marching band in high school, as section leader for the piccolos," says Valerie Coleman. "Marching band is huge in Kentucky, where I grew up. We'd compete against other bands. It was intense." All that marching helped her become a better musician. "We worked a lot on memorization and on marching and playing at the same time. Marching helps you develop an internal rhythm."

She had started playing flute in fourth grade with group lessons at school and continued with school band classes until the end of high school. "I had great band directors." They drilled kids in how to identify musical intervals, such as perfect fourths and fifths. "That developed my ear," she says, making it easy to figure out notes in pop tunes she heard on the radio or in theme songs for *Jeopardy* and other TV shows. "I'd sing the tunes in my head and write them down so I could play them. I was good at practicing those things, the cool things, but getting me to practice scales was like pulling teeth." She started making up her own pieces and writing them down. "It was a hobby."

In tenth grade, her band director persuaded her that it was time to take her playing to a new level by studying with a private teacher at a local university. Through those lessons she learned classical pieces—and played scales more regularly. She went on to major in music at college where she focused on flute and also on that "hobby" she had of writing music. Now, as a flutist who also composes, she still uses the good ear she began developing in band. "I'm influenced by things I hear—a car horn, a phrase a jazz musician plays, something on the radio—and try to get those sounds and their emotions down on paper."

Look Around

If talking things over with the teacher doesn't help, there's always another solution: Try to switch to another teacher. That may even be possible at your regular school if there's more than one music teacher in the district. However, if another teacher isn't available and you can't switch, consider the advice of Mike, who plays viola: "Ignore the negatives. Pick what good things they have to say."

With private lessons outside of school, it's a different story. "I was not making any progress with my private teacher, so I got a new teacher," reports Ethan, a sax player. So did Ann, who explains, "My first piano teacher made it clear who her favorite students were and the rest of us got very discouraged. I found a new teacher who had more confidence in me." Matt, a trombonist, says, "If you have a private teacher who isn't your type musically, find someone who is."

For some teens, a teacher switch happens just because it's time for a change. "My first piano teacher taught mainly young children. There came a time when she couldn't be helpful to me anymore," says Tammy. "That teacher understood when I signed up with a new teacher." You and a teacher may also part ways if you find you have different goals. For instance, a student may want to play only jazz, but the teacher may prefer to teach classical music.

A Winning Theory

Besides instrument lessons, some teens also take classes in music theory at regular school, music school, camp, or with a private teacher. Learning music theory means finding out how different chords and scales are put together, how to count different rhythms, and what different marks on a score mean—well worth learning, according to our teen advisors. "If you understand what chord is being played, you can place your own note better," notes Allison, a French horn player. Katherine adds, "It helped my sight-reading because I can see the notes as parts of chords or scales rather than just difficulties that I can't play." Randy, who plays jazz, pop, funk, and classical, points out, "Theory helped me understand chord progressions, improvisation, and harmony."

Spotlight On...

DANIEL KATZEN— French Horn

Take It: "I had a tyrannical band director in high school," recalls Daniel Katzen, French horn player with the Boston Symphony. "He was excellent, but he'd embarrass kids and came down on them if they played a wrong note. That was enough to break a lot of people. It hardened me. I was able to take it. I felt good enough about what I was doing that if I missed a note or someone made fun of me, inside I'd say to myself, 'You know, I don't really care what he thinks.' I knew I was pretty good. I wasn't great, but I knew I wasn't terrible either." He feels part of what helped him not get crushed by tough conductors was that he was so crazy about music. "I also played string bass, kept up with piano, and picked up recorder, too. I was always putting together brass quintets or jazz groups with my friends. That's what told me I was going to be a musician. I loved playing music. I hated practicing, but I loved playing."

Conductor Blues

Many of the skills that help in getting along with teachers also help in smoothing out a relationship with a conductor. Our teen advisors report that most conductors they've dealt with have been very supportive and good about making kids feel great and play well. But Kristen has also met the other kind. "Sometimes you get a very intimidating conductor and you sit in utter fear," warns this singer. Other kids gripe about conductors who "always pick the same people to do solos," "never pay attention to our section," or "are too bossy." Even pros complain that some conductors are hard to take.

You usually can't go out shopping for a new conductor as you can with a private teacher. If you want to play in the band or orchestra you're in, you have to find ways to deal with even the most temperamental conductor. Here are our teens' tips for coping.

"Usually conductors are demanding when they know you can do better."

"With yelling conductors, I just smile and cooperate," says Elizabeth, a cellist. That's a smart move even with non-shouters. As Stephanie, a clarinetist, notes, "It's important to do what's asked without complaint. Usually conductors want to help you do your best."

"Conducting is hard," explains Matt, a trombonist. "Sometimes you have to adjust." After all, getting a bunch of kids to pull off a great performance isn't easy, especially when the kids are at all different levels. During rehearsal, the conductor's word is law, just as with a coach of a sports team. But after rehearsal, there's room to negotiate.

"Don't be afraid to talk with them. If something is wrong, let them know," advises Mike, a viola player. Joe, a percussionist, agrees, "Don't argue or talk back during rehearsal, but come back later and state your problem like an adult." This approach has worked for Stephanie, who remembers, "One time when I thought I wasn't being respected, I talked with the conductor and played for her. Soon I was getting better parts." Emily was frustrated by a conductor who kept ignoring her section—the horns. "I finally told him how I felt and after that he paid a lot more attention to us," she explains.

If you're shy, try Elizabeth's strategy. "I wrote the conductor a letter and he agreed and made things different," explains this violinist. Or get back-up support, as Nobu-Ann did. "I talked to the conductor with my mother and we explained what bothered me about how the orchestra was run," this violinist recalls.

"Develop a good relationship with the conductor outside rehearsals," suggests Alan, a cellist. "Then you can ask to be considered for solo parts." Andrea, a bassoonist, adds, "Even if a conductor is hard on you, don't give up. Think about how to improve. Usually conductors are demanding when they know you can do better."

How Not to Get on a Conductor's Nerves

♦ "Stop when they say, 'Stop!' Don't keep playing. That aggravates them and makes them yell."
—*Shannon, flute*
♦ "Don't have arguments with fellow musicians."
—*Allison, French horn*
♦ "Practice your part so you make the most of rehearsal time. Conductors get frustrated when students come unprepared."
—*Ben, oboe*
♦ "Listen. Conductors don't like repeating what they've said. It wastes rehearsal time."
—*Emily, French horn*
♦ "Work with them. Conductors have a lot to deal with."
—*Dave, trumpet*
♦ "Smile. Never yawn in front of them."
—*Andrea, flute*
♦ "If you know your music, they'll respect you."
—*Kristen, singer*

Gear Up

9

EVEN THE BEST musician can be undone by poor equipment. Our advisors tell how to hunt down a super instrument, what to do if it starts giving you aches and pains, how to make the most of high-tech electronic gear that can help musicians, plus how to make pesky music books stay open to the right page.

Instrument Hunting

"A good way to find an instrument is to get advice first from music teachers or from older, more experienced players," advises Rachel, a violinist. That's a wise move whether you rent, buy, or borrow an instrument. Learning to play is tricky enough without struggling with troublesome gear. All those shiny instruments in a store seem wonderful, but some may be duds. A teacher or other expert can help point you toward brands, models, and sizes that will work best for you. Many of our teen advisors have a teacher try an instrument before deciding on it—a good plan to follow whenever possible. Teacher advice can also help with extras, such as a music stand, or that all-important time machine, a metronome.

Freebies

There are several ways of coming up with an instrument. Freebies, of course, are the least expensive way to go. Paula Robison started out as a kid with a freebie when she borrowed an old flute from a family friend. Several of our teen advisors also began on freebies, using instruments passed along to them from family or friends, or ones their schools lent out for free. A freebie can be a great deal if the instrument works well. But if a teacher checks it out and turns thumbs down, search for a better choice.

Renting

Many teens rented their first instrument from school, from a music store, or from a dealer (a person or business that handles instruments from certain manufacturers). Ask a teacher which stores or dealers in your area offer good quality rentals. If possible, rent a new instrument, not a used one. If you rent a used one, have a teacher check it over if possible to be sure it's clean and in good condition. Make sure the store will do repairs if anything breaks during normal use. Also, see if the store has an option-to-buy plan, which can give you a price break if you buy an instrument later, either the rental or a new one.

Be sure you can exchange the instrument for another if it doesn't work well. When Noah rented a used tenor sax, he couldn't make a sound on it at the store. He thought he was used to playing an alto and didn't yet have the knack of handling a tenor. At his next lesson, his teacher couldn't make a sound on that old tenor either. Back it went to the store to be exchanged for one that worked.

The Buying Game

After renting for a year or so, many teens bought an instrument, usually asking teachers for help in sorting through the wide range of choices. "My teacher recommended a store and a specific trombone model," reports Gary. Allison says her teacher "had me try out three different French horns and I picked the one I liked best." Cie Ann's teacher went violin shopping with her. Pete knew what kind of marimba he wanted not only from his teacher's advice but also "from hearing so many different models at music school." Using a computer to visit instrument manufacturers' Web sites can also help in learning about the variety of models that are available.

Where did the teens buy? Some shopped at music stores. "Go to a big store and try out lots of different brands to see which one sounds best," suggests Tammy, a flutist. There are also other places to try. Malena bought her French horn through her school. Karen reports, "My violin teacher sells violins, so he sold me a good one." Josh bought his trombone through a mail-order catalog, after checking at stores first. Daniel found a good deal on a French horn through an Internet Web site that specializes in horns. If you buy through the Internet, make sure the seller will let you ship the instrument back if, after playing it for a trial period, you discover you don't like it. Some musicians also find good deals at conventions of music organizations. Ask your teacher or an older musician friend if any conventions will be held in your area.

Carrie's grandfather helped in her search for a marimba. "At first I played the school's marimba, staying after school every day for two years to practice," she says. "Then, my grandfather put an ad in the newspaper asking if anyone had one in their attic. A man called with a great marimba. We bought it."

Used instruments like the one Carrie bought often cost less than new ones and may be good. However, new ones usually have the advantage of a warranty—a promise by the store or manufacturer to repair the instrument for a certain period if it breaks as a result of normal playing. Used instruments bought at a store may sometimes have a warranty, but if you buy a used model privately (not at a store or dealer) you're on your own for repairs.

Money Help: "When my mother couldn't afford to buy me a saxophone, the schools provided one at almost no cost," recalls pro Joshua Redman (shown here at around age 11). Many schools lend instruments for free or make special deals if a student can't afford rental fees. In some areas, people donate used instruments for students to use. Talk with your school's teacher or call a nearby music school.

Clean Up Your Act

"Keep your instrument clean," advises Daniel, a trombonist. If it sounds fuzzy, maybe it's dirty. But before you clean up your act: Stop! Get instructions from your teacher or a music store. Better yet, watch an expert do a cleaning, as well as a regular maintenance (oiling, waxing, greasing, or changing strings, reeds, and pads). Then you'll know what to do and won't get fouled up as Danny did. He warns fellow string players, "Do NOT remove all four strings at the same time in order to clean dust from under the bridge. Take my word for it. Not a good idea!" With all the strings off, the bridge may fall, making it mighty tricky to get everything lined up again.

"A big problem with string instruments is kids don't store them properly," notes Aaron Bodling, who repaired instruments for a music store in Eastchester, New York. "It they're stored in a place that's too humid, too dry, too hot, or too cold, the wood frame can warp. Also, don't leave them out in a car when it's very cold or very hot. They're fragile." Of course, extreme heat and cold aren't great for other instruments either. There are many do's and don'ts in caring for an instrument. Ask your teacher for the details and for the name of a good repair shop or a reliable piano tuner.

Spotlight On...

DAVID BRAGUNIER— Tuba

In Tune: David Bragunier, former principal tuba player with the National Symphony, learned the hard way to get expert advice before buying an instrument. He entered the world of tubas as a seventh grader when he volunteered to play his school's sousaphone (the huge curly tuba). His family couldn't afford to buy one. So he used school instruments. When he applied to go to Peabody Conservatory after high school, he auditioned on a sousaphone that belonged to his high school. He got accepted. That's when he had to scrape together the money to buy his first tuba. "I went to a music store in Baltimore. They brought out a couple of tubas," he recalls. "I bought the one I thought sounded best. But when I took my first lesson at Peabody, the teacher said, 'That tuba is too out of tune. You have to get a new one.'" Before heading back to the store, he got advice on picking a better horn. "The store let me trade in for a new tuba. All's well that ends well."

Book It

Musical books and scores aren't "gear" exactly. But they need care, too, so they'll last and won't flop shut at all the wrong moments:

- ◆ "Get a metal stand with clips to hold the pages open."
  —*Tammy, flute*
- ◆ "Fold back the book's binding to make it stay open."
  — *Stephanie, flute*
- ◆ "Use clothes pins (or plastic clips) to make the book stay open. They're clunky and can get in the way, but they work!"
  — *Joel, violin, piano*
- ◆ "Have your music books rebound with spiral binding at a stationery store. For a few dollars you can save a lot of aggravation. Spiral-bound books stay open better."
  — *Gary, trombone*
- ◆ "Duct tape the edges of the covers, to make them last longer."
  — *Lauren, double bass*
- ◆ "Tape the pages together so they can unfold like a book (if your music is on loose pages)."
  — *RoseLee, violin*

Ouch Relief

Of course, one of the most important things to keep in good working order is: YOU! If you get aches and pains from playing an instrument, chances are you're doing something wrong. That's what Andrea discovered. "Sometimes my mouth and wrists would hurt after practicing a long time on bassoon," she notes. A few other teens report having pains now and then while practicing. Most discussed the situation with their teachers to track down the cause.

Andrea has found her muscle pains go away if she takes rest breaks during practicing. "My bassoon teacher always says to take a break when anything becomes painful," Andrea explains. "Your body is warning you that you need to rest a while." Experts agree this is one of the best ways to prevent muscle problems. "When kids get to the point where they practice more than an hour a day, they need to take breaks every half hour or hour," recommends Dr. Ralph Manchester, an expert in performing arts medicine who works with music students at the Eastman School of Music.

As violinist Joshua Bell notes, "If things start to hurt, stop and give it a rest. Don't push yourself when your arm starts to hurt." Or your fingers, lips, back, or anything else. Breaks are especially important for wind and brass players. If they play for too long a stretch, they can mess up their "embouchure" (the technical word for the position lips have to be in to play a wind or brass instrument). Some brass experts recommend a 15-minute break after 45 minutes of practicing.

Hold It Right

Alyssa's muscle aches come when "I hold my violin incorrectly." Poor technique is a major cause of muscle pain. Claire, an oboist, suggests, "Look in a mirror and watch yourself play. Some people play in a strange position unconsciously and this causes pain."

"Sometimes I videotape students so they can see what they're doing," says flute teacher Vanessa Breault Mulvey. "The best way to improve is to see what needs fixing. A big part of my teaching is showing students how the body moves so they can move correctly when playing. There's a great desire when you practice to keep going, to say, 'I've got to get through this.' You get sucked into what I call the tunnel of music, blocking everything else out, not noticing how your body feels. In this 'tunnel,' you tense your muscles and that affects every part of your body, as well as your sound and musicality." During lessons, she stops students every few minutes to do a musical check and a body check, too, asking: "Were you happy with your sound? Were your lips overly tight? Were you aware of your hands as you played? Was your head balanced on your spine as you played or did it move off balance?" This encourages students to do the same kind of self-checking when practicing at home.

Some pros who didn't fix ouch-causing problems soon enough and who practice many, *many* hours a day have developed injuries that interfere with their playing. "This doesn't happen to most kids through the high school level because they usually aren't practicing enough yet to make such injuries happen," says Dr. Ralph Manchester. How can teens and pre-teens prevent future injuries? Dr. Manchester recommends, "Pay attention to what the teacher tells you about using good technique. Try to stay relaxed when you practice, and take breaks. When you have a performance coming up, don't suddenly increase your practicing by a great amount. That's a common cause for pain."

Pro violinist Peter Oundjian adds, "Find a teacher who has a very flexible method, who understands the importance of encouraging you to use your muscles in the most efficient way possible." Mr. Oundjian developed a performance-related injury as an adult after many years of a heavy performance and rehearsal schedule as first violinist with the Tokyo String Quartet. That injury caused him to shift from playing violin to being a conductor. He also suggests doing some stretching exercises before playing, "just like a soccer coach would have you do. Warm up your body slowly." Malena's horn teacher taught her "breathing exercises to help me relax before and after I play." This has helped end the muscle cramps she used to get from being too tense while playing. Ask your teacher about techniques to help you relax.

If your teacher can't help you get rid of aches and pains, your family may want to talk with some experts. A music school may be able to help, or check out the Web site of the Performing Arts Medicine Association. (See this book's Resource Guide.)

Braces: The metal wires that light up many kids' smiles can present challenges for some musicians. Tammy says that after getting braces it took a few days to adjust to the new way her mouth felt as she played flute. It took Cie Ann about a month to get the hang of playing clarinet with braces. For brass players, it can take longer—even several months to adjust. "At first, I couldn't play as high as I wanted and my lips got cut," recalls Daniel, a trombonist. Katherine, a trumpeter, adds, "Braces made my tone very airy at first. Don't get discouraged. Keep practicing and it gets better."

"Lips toughen up in time," notes Dr. Christopher Carpenter, a Denver orthodontist. "If someone is having a hard time, there are little plastic bumper guards you can get from the orthodontist that clip onto the braces. They cover the braces to make them smooth so it's more comfortable when you play an instrument." What about using wax to cover braces? "The wax tends to fall off. Bumper guards stay on better," he says. Allison, a horn player, points out, "Braces aren't forever. It's nice when they come off!"

Wiped Out

Another ouch-causer: a long marathon rehearsal that comes right before a concert. How can you do your best if you're wiped out? Here's how Maria Beatriz, a pianist, copes when she's exhausted. "I go to a separate room where I can be alone for a couple of minutes," she says. "I mentally start a recovery of my body strength and keep thinking positive thoughts, thinking I'm *not* tired. I let the music flow back to my fingers." Lauren, a double bass player, adds, "Massage your hands. Then let your arms dangle at your sides." Joel's advice for fellow-violinists: "Sit down and take a few deep breaths and then start warming up with slow, easy exercises."

Wind and brass players need to be especially careful, because hours and hours of rehearsal can temporarily mess up their lips. Claire recalls, "At all-state, we had nonstop rehearsals all weekend. I was playing first oboe. By the time we got to the concert, I could barely play."

What if lips start to go? "The way to get them back is to rest. Ice doesn't help," advises pro trumpeter Barbara Butler. "Resting them overnight is best. If you can't do that, rest for as long as you can. If you have to rehearse, say quietly to the conductor, 'If I give it all now, I won't have it for tonight. Let me just play a little bit now.' That's hard to do if your friends are blasting their brains out because they don't have the high first-trumpet part. Singers call it 'marking.' They stand up there for dress rehearsals and sing part voice."

Flute teacher Vanessa Breault Mulvey has similar advice for flutists: "If you're in a rehearsal and have to go right into a concert, play comfortably but don't try to do too much. All that muscle work can take a lot out of your lips." Pro horn player Daniel Katzen agrees, "Never blow or play so much in rehearsal that it hurts. Of course, you'll never grow if you don't play, get tired, and play some more. You have to know how much farther to push without hurting yourself."

Gearing Up Online

A computer is another piece of equipment many musicians find helpful, especially because it provides access to a lot of information about music that can be found on the Internet. Courtney, a bass trombonist, uses her computer to hunt for musical goodies on Internet search engines, such as Google or Yahoo. "I use the Internet to research musicians and conductors, and to read the background on composers and pieces I'm learning," she says. When she finds recordings she likes, she buys them by downloading them from Internet stores such as iTunes. This can be a money-saver, allowing her to buy only pieces she likes on an album rather than shelling out for the whole CD.

"Having access to so much music online is great for being a well-rounded musician," says violinist Hilary Hahn. "I use the Internet to listen to a fair amount of folk, trip hop [a kind of British hip hop], rock, and world music. Listening to any kind of music informs your perspective. With a rap song, for instance, figure out why you like it and how to translate that energy into your playing."

In addition, on sites such as YouTube there are videos to watch online of performances by all kinds of musicians, from violinist Jascha Heifetz and other legends of the past to most of the pros featured in this book. There are also videos of quite a few amateurs and students, too, and even one showing a trumpet-playing robot. "I encourage kids to watch these videos," says flute teacher Vanessa Breault Mulvey. "I caution them that there are some awesome performances online and some really bad ones, too. Use your objectivity to assess the performance, the phrasing, how they look as they play. Determine what works well and why." Sometimes whole concerts are online. The New York and Los Angeles Philharmonic orchestras have posted podcasts of concerts that can be downloaded for free. The Boston Pops has recorded special performances just for broadcast on its Web site.

Also fun is discovering sheet music online. Violin teacher Rebecca Henry had two students who wanted a different kind of duet. They searched online and found an arrangement for two violins of a piece that's normally for band: "Stars and Stripes Forever." It didn't come from a big publisher but directly from the person who did the arrangement. Ms. Henry's students have also downloaded scores for pieces they're working on with her in their lessons. "Sometimes I don't like that because I prefer certain editions, but it's a way for them to start practicing a piece until they find the edition I like."

Courtney likes to search online for MIDI files to download. These files let you hear music on a computer and see the notes, too, if the computer has music-writing software such as Finale, Sibelius, Freestyle, Encore, Cakewalk, Garage Band, or some other notation program.

Other online goodies include sites that offer music lessons, teach music theory, or show how to play cool guitar solos. Some professional musicians, including Hilary Hahn, have blogs on their Web sites and chat away online about performing, touring, or life in general. The Resource Guide at the end of this book lists a few music-related Web sites.

Recording Options

"I have used a cassette tape recorder to record myself playing," says John, a teen French horn player. He has also used a newer type of recorder—a digital one—that makes an audio recording that can be

entered onto a computer. There are lots of different options for making recordings. The one to use depends on your budget and your reason for making a recording.

If you're recording your lesson so you can remember what your teacher said, a small, inexpensive handheld recorder is fine, either tape or digital. Some students use their iPods or mp3 players to make these informal recordings.

However, if you plan to use a recording to enter a competition or to audition for a school or summer program, you want a setup that produces a higher quality sound than a small tape player delivers. Some students record by plugging a digital microphone right into a computer that has special music software. Newer computers may come already loaded with that kind of software, or you could install programs such as Garage Band or Cakewalk. Another option is to plug a microphone into another device—an audio interface—which then plugs into a computer. Interfaces, such as those from M-Audio, may produce a better-quality sound. Recording setups like these can be expensive and complicated to run. Plus, equipment and software keep changing. Your music teacher or the tech department at your school may already have snazzy equipment you can use. If you'd rather beef up your own home system, ask teachers for advice first. Then quiz sales people at electronic and music stores. As with buying a new instrument: Try before you buy.

Recording Warnings

Wu Han knows about recordings, having started a recording company, ArtistLed, with her husband, cellist David Finckel. She also knows about the audition CDs that students make. She has listened to lots of them as a judge on jury panels for school applications and competitions. "The quality of the recording is so important," she says. "Many times judges put on a student's CD and it sounds like it was recorded in the bathroom. You can hardly hear any notes. Or the piano is so out of tune we can't listen to it. We can't judge such a CD. It's difficult to select a candidate who submits a CD like that. It doesn't show professionalism. Judges put an application like that aside. You have to have a certain quality to the recording before a judge can give you an opportunity." She recommends:

♦ "Make sure the instrument is in tune. That's basic."
♦ "Do some investigative work on the selection of a microphone and recording equipment. A good digital mike is pretty inexpensive these days."
♦ "Experiment with the location of the microphone when you record. Don't record with the mike very far away from you in a big hall so you don't hear any detail. But you don't want the mike too close either so the sound is ugly. Definitely don't put the mike on the music stand so every time you play the stand shakes and makes noise. Silly things like that decrease your chance of being considered."
♦ "Aim as close to a professional recording quality as possible."

Music-Writing Gear

Software that lets you write—notate—music can also be a big help, and not just for would-be composers. Thanks to her music-writing software, Courtney can play a piece she downloads as a MIDI file even if

it wasn't written for her instrument, bass trombone. The software lets the notes from the piece appear on her computer screen. Then her notation software lets her change the notes to the right key for trombone. Sometimes she arranges pieces she downloads so her trombone choir can play them. She has also found a rather unusual use for her notation software. "I use it as a metronome. I have it write out 500 measures of quarter notes and put the playback on repeat six times." The software lets her change how fast the computer plays those measures.

The playback function on notation programs is also great for learning a new piece. If Courtney downloads the score for a brass quintet, she can tell the computer to play just her trombone part, to help her hear it better. Max does this, too, and has also used the software for its main purpose: to write pieces of his own. He feels that writing music "just for fun," as he does, helps him learn more about chords and harmony. The playback function lets him hear what he writes. Plus, the computer can create a MIDI sound file of the piece, which he can use to burn a CD of his computer playing his piece. He can also e-mail that MIDI file to friends.

Some notation software is easy to use, such as Garage Band, which lets you write a tune and then perk it up by adding ready-to-use back-up rhythms and sounds. You can also "create your own virtual onstage band and play along on your favorite instrument," according to the Garage Band Web site.

Other notation programs are more advanced and harder to master, such as two of the most widely used: Finale and Sibelius. Both have introductory versions to download free—Finale Notepad and Sibelius Scorch—but even so, it helps to have a teacher show you how to find your way around these two. Other notation programs include Encore, Freestyle, and Cakewalk, to name a few, as well as the more complex Pro Tools and Digital Performer. There's a wide price range among programs and big differences in what the programs can do.

If you're tempted to give some a try, check with music teachers first. Many are quite tech savvy. Rebecca Henry uses Sibelius to write warms-ups for her violin students at Peabody. She also takes vocal music and arranges it for violin. Amy Rosen, an elementary school orchestra teacher in Larchmont, New York, mastered Finale, although she admits it was a struggle. She stuck with it so she could pull out one part, such as the viola part, from any score she had on her computer and then create a MIDI file of just that part for her students to hear. Tom Jordan, another

Larchmont teacher, does this, too, not only with published scores, but also with pieces he arranges for his middle-school band. He has also set up a blog on which students share opinions of music they've heard and upload recordings of their playing so he can offer suggestions.

Spotlight On...

JOHN ADAMS—Composing & Clarinet

Finding Your Way: "Finding your own voice as a composer takes time," says Pulitzer Prize winner John Adams. "The first piece I consider a real 'John Adams piece' is one I wrote when I was 29. You can't expect to have a mature, unique voice as a composer as a kid. Mozart was able to write masterpieces at age 18 because he wrote in the accepted style of his time, just doing it better than anyone else. Now, composers are expected to create their own style. It's a huge challenge. I experimented with different styles. It came gradually."

His experimenting began early. "Most young kids are very creative but many give up because they're not encouraged," he notes. Luckily, he received loads of encouragement. His parents, amateur musicians, started him on clarinet in second grade. Then, when his third grade teacher read the class a biography of Mozart, that helped give him the idea of writing his own music. Soon, he was doing so—in his imagination. While walking around his New Hampshire town delivering newspapers, he dreamed up pieces for orchestras to play. He didn't write them down. He didn't know how yet. But by age 10, he wrote a piece for just one instrument, a harpsichord. Before long, his parents found a teacher to give him composition lessons. By age 14, he wrote his first orchestral piece, which a local orchestra played. The audience loved it. Even though audience members were patients at a psychiatric hospital, he still found this "very encouraging."

He was also doing lots of listening to classical, jazz, and later to rock. He took out scores from the library, reading them while listening to recordings "to develop a knowledge of what's possible." He kept up with clarinet, playing in orchestras through college, where he majored in music. When composing during college and after, he experimented with new musical styles, such as electronic music and minimalism (with its pulsating, repeating rhythms). He kept picking and choosing among styles until at last he hit on his way of composing, his own special voice.

High-Tech vs. Low-Tech Composing

"Computers can be very limiting," warns Pulitzer Prize-winning composer John Adams. "They are useful tools for composers. I use computers myself. Almost all composers use them now. I love electronics and adore changing sounds with software programs that let you do that. The problem is that computers are machines. They are mechanical and automatic, as machines are. Composers who use only computers tend to compose what works well on the machine—using regular rhythms and harmonies. It discourages you from being radical in your thinking. I can tell almost immediately if a piece was composed only on a computer. I recommend that students first plan things out with pencil and paper, and input it into the computer later."

He had a young student who was writing exciting pieces by hand until he bought notation software and began composing only on computer. "His pieces were losing some of their imagination and charm. I told him to go back to pencil and paper, try things at the piano, and then when it's ready, enter it into the notation program. He did. The difference was amazing."

Another drawback: The playback function on notation programs "doesn't accurately reflect how instruments really sound," says Judah Adashi, a composer who teaches at Peabody. "You need to develop your ear so you know how instruments sound in different registers. I've had students use these programs to write orchestra pieces that seem impressive, but a lot of times they just came up with a melody line, some harmony, and then did a lot of cutting and pasting without thinking about how it will sound. Is the flute really going to carry if it's played in such a low register?" He encourages students to start by writing for just one instrument, really learning about that instrument and what it can do. "Strike a balance with the technology," advises Mr. Adashi. "I do a lot of sketching by hand first. But there comes a point where it's reasonable to move to the computer, which can then bring up new possibilities you hadn't thought of."

Of course, notation programs have a big plus: neatly printed scores. "You don't want to give performers a handwritten score," he warns. Erika Nickrenz of the Eroica Trio agrees: "We used to have to read what seemed like chicken scratching when we got new pieces from composers. Now they print them out on computers, a huge improvement."

More Tips for Would-Be Composers

♦ **Play well.** "Play at least one instrument really well," advises John Adams. He recommends learning an orchestra instrument because "being in orchestras is a good way to learn what other instruments can do." He played clarinet well enough that as an undergraduate at

Harvard he sometimes performed with the Boston Symphony when it needed an extra clarinetist. Composer Steven Mackey adds that you want to get good enough on an instrument so you can improvise. That way when you compose, "your body can lead you to something your mind wouldn't think of." When he reaches a spot in a piece where he needs to add a solo line, he often improvises on his main instrument, guitar, even if the part isn't for guitar. "I play around with the material on guitar and find something."

♦ **Piano, please**. "Piano is helpful for a composer because you learn to think vertically as well as horizontally," says Mr. Adams. Being able to play many notes at once up and down the keyboard helps you create chords and harmonies to go with your melody line. "I never took piano lessons, but I don't recommend that. We just never had a piano at home until I was in eighth or ninth grade." He taught himself to play and uses piano to compose. So does Mr. Mackey, who took piano lessons in college. "You don't have to be great at it, but piano is really handy."

♦ **Know the score.** "Listen to everything," says Mr. Adams, from classical to jazz and rock. "Read scores, too." Mr. Adashi has students listen to and read scores for pieces that feature instruments they're composing for in order to "think about what the instrument can do, where it sounds best. Meet with people who play the instrument. Have them play a bit and talk about what works well on the instrument and what doesn't."

♦ **Patience**. "Don't be discouraged if you can't notate intricate rhythms right away," says Mr. Adashi. As Mr. Adams notes, "Being a composer is like being a gardener. If you do it every day and know what to water, what to fertilize, what to prune, what to weed out, the composition will grow almost on its own."

Other Gadgets

There are lots of other gadgets that can help a young musician, such as electronic tuners and metronomes. "They're all pretty much the same, and not too expensive," says violin teacher Amy Rosen. However, there's another item she likes that is more pricey: a CD player that can slow down a piece without changing the pitch. She uses it during lessons and for practice purposes so she can slow down play-along CDs, to give students the idea of playing slower during the learning stage. Courtney, who has also used one of these CD players, feels that slowing down the music "lets you listen better to the line of a piece, the phrasing, tuning, and technique." There are software programs that can do this too, such as the Amazing Slow Downer, one of several that can be found by hunting on Internet search engines. However, a young trumpeter reports having a less-than-wonderful experience using such a program to transcribe a jazz piece. Once again, the best advice is—you guessed it—try before you buy.

If Only

What teens wish they'd known when they were younger about dealing with their gear:

♦ "Hold the violin up. It makes the sound carry. Think of the instrument as an extension of your body."
   — *Karen, violin*

♦ "Keep your flute up straight when you play. If you hold it pointing down, the sound doesn't carry or come out as well."
   — *Stephanie, flute*

♦ "Breathe from your stomach muscles (not from your chest or shoulders). It helps so much."
   — *Sarah, French horn*

♦ "Come prepared: Always have a pencil, extra strings, rosin, mutes, reeds, etc., with you in your case."
   — *Jenny, violin*

♦ "Percussion players should have extra sticks and mallets. I've broken sticks during performances more times than I can count."
   — *Eric, percussion*

♦ "If it's cold, bring gloves to put on before a performance. Your fingers can't function to their best ability when they're cold."
   — *Anne, bassoon, sax*

♦ "Be careful with cellos when going up or down stairs. Don't walk around with your endpin out. That's just asking for trouble."
   — *Wendy, cello*

Play On

10

"**H**AVE FUN WITH your instrument and stick with it!" urges Claire. This enthusiastic oboist points out, "Even if you don't become a professional musician, music is something you can always keep with you throughout your life." Some of our troupe of teen advisors reported dreaming about becoming pros. Others aimed for different careers, such as becoming doctors, psychologists, teachers, sports lawyers, public relations specialists, and even ambassadors. Whatever their careers, their experience with music will probably help them. Chances are they'll find ways to keep making music no matter what their day jobs. Read on for ways to keep the beat going.

Bragging Rights

"Playing an instrument helps academically with other subjects," claims Muh-Huey. This is something many of our teen advisors have noticed. She feels the time she put into mastering piano and violin has been time well spent.

Don't just take her word for it. Check out recent scores on the SAT (Scholastic Aptitude Test), the test students take when applying to college. In 2001, students who had experience performing music tended to score higher than average on both the verbal and math sections of the SAT. So did those who took courses in other arts areas, such as drama, art, or dance. Maybe music helps students do better, or perhaps teens who study music tend to be disciplined and serious about learning, which rubs off in other subjects as well. Education researchers have also noticed connections between music and learning. For example, a study in California found that preschoolers who took music lessons improved in their spatial reasoning skills, which play a part in learning math. In another study, older students improved in spatial reasoning after listening to Mozart.

Experts don't know exactly why music may help with other subjects. Muh-Huey feels music aided her because "it teaches you how to manage time, how to manage stress, and how to memorize things quickly." Being in ensembles also teaches teamwork skills that will come in handy later in the world of work.

Adults who studied music as kids and went on to have other careers often feel their musical training gave them a big boost. Dr. Yeou-Cheng Ma, the sister of cellist Yo-Yo Ma, is a pediatrician who plays violin and viola. She notes, "A lot of music training is memory training. The more you train the memory, the more your neurons connect, and that's good for anything."

Spotlight On...

YEOU-CHENG MA— Medicine & Violin

Pass It On: "For me, music is like breathing. It's not a question of how I find the time to play. I need music to balance myself," says Dr. Yeou-Cheng Ma, a pediatrician who has been playing violin since she was a little girl. Unlike her brother, Yo-Yo Ma, she decided not to have a performing career. The competitive stress of a pro's life didn't seem to suit her, but music is still a major part of her life. On weekends, she and her husband run a music school and youth orchestra in Manhasset, New York—the Children's Orchestra Society. "We encourage kids not to compete against each other but against their past selves, to improve compared to yesterday," says Dr. Ma. She still plays violin as much as she can. Even in medical school she played chamber music with friends. "We'd do gigs. I still do that. My husband plays guitar and we play duets."

Which Way?

The road ahead is long and bumpy, with unexpected twists and turns. It's hard for young people to know where their paths will lead. When Richard Stoltzman was a teen, he thought he'd probably become a dentist. In college, he majored in math, and also music. He applied to go to dental school after college. But when he visited the dental school for an interview, the medical atmosphere made him uncomfortable. "Whereas when I was at a music school, I was always happy," he recalls. That's when he realized how important music was to him.

So instead of dental school, he enrolled in a graduate school program in clarinet playing at Yale.

Dr. Eugene Beresin's path led the other way. He was a music major in college who dreamed of being a pianist. He also took science courses in case he decided to go to medical school. For a while he did both—went to medical school and played gigs (performances). "The business side of music, the grind of trying to get jobs, kind of ruined music for me," he recalls. He shifted to medicine, became a psychiatrist, but never totally gave up piano. He now plays with a few jazz bands on evenings and weekends.

He is glad he spent time as a kid learning piano and guitar. It gave him skills he uses now. "I don't have time to practice much now. If I'm lucky, I touch the piano two or three times a week," he says. "As a kid, I had time to sit at the piano for hours trying to learn a tune. Once you've done that—learned the basics—it's like riding a bike. You can always go back to it. It's important to help kids enjoy what they're doing in music so they'll put in the time at the instrument. So they can learn the language." And keep their options open.

Pressure Cooker

Pressure on kids can get pretty intense—the pressure to do well in school, do well in sports, do well in music. Sometimes it's just too much. That's when kids might think of quitting music. "It's important to help them figure out where the instrument fits into their life," says violin teacher Rebecca Henry. "Some kids say, 'I'd like to quit but my mom won't let me.' I talk with the mom and say maybe it isn't so horrible if they quit. Maybe they can have music in their life some other way. Maybe they can let it go for a while and come back to it later on their own terms."

She notes that there's also a less drastic way to solve the pressure-cooker problem: Some kids decide they don't have to be great at everything. That might mean dropping other activities to focus on music, or lightening up on music, to keep playing but without so much pressure. "For some, that frees them up so they can really start to enjoy their instrument again," notes Ms. Henry.

Conquering the "Can'ts"

Even though becoming a pro is tough, many teens follow their dreams and give it a try. To do so, they and their teachers have to plot a careful course of what pieces to learn, what camps and schools to apply to, which competitions to enter. It also helps to find a way to cope with the "can'ts"—the discouraging comments and experiences that are bound to pop up, remarks like: "Oh, *you* can't do that. No way." Conquering the "can'ts" involves finding ways to keep up your morale so a less-than-marvelous performance doesn't knock you down. "Pick yourself up, dust yourself off, and say, 'Okay, I can learn from this,'" observes flutist Paula Robison.

Wynton Marsalis has had to deal with his share of "can'ts." When he was a teen, people warned him he couldn't do well in both classical and jazz trumpet. He proved them wrong, winning several Grammy awards for both his classical and jazz albums, as well as the Pulitzer Prize for one of his compositions. "Some people will always try to discourage you, but a lot of people will try to help you, too," notes Mr. Marsalis. "It all depends on what you give the most attention to. A lot of people say bad stuff about you, but a lot say good stuff. For some reason, we gravitate toward that bad stuff. You're not going to be unanimously accepted and loved. You're not going to be unanimously vilified (disliked) either. Choose what you gravitate toward. You have to try to find your own way."

Spotlight On...

MARIN ALSOP— Conducting & Violin

Never Say Never: "Girls don't do that." That's what nine-year-old Marin Alsop heard in 1965 when she told her violin teacher she wanted to be a conductor. She had fallen in love with conduct- ing at a concert for kids con- ducted by Leonard Bernstein. "He was so enthusiastic, so into the music, having so much fun," she recalls. She didn't let her teacher's comment get her down, even though her teacher had a point: There were few female conductors back then. In fact, no woman was ever chief conductor of a major U.S. orchestra until Marin Alsop won such a job with the Baltimore Symphony—40 years after her teacher's discourag- ing remark.

The road to the top wasn't easy. Her parents, both musicians, were supportive. Her father even bought young Marin a box of batons. But it was a long time before she used them. "I realized conducting requires a lot of knowledge of music," she says. She set out first to learn all she could. She kept on with violin, while also studying the complete orchestral scores for pieces her music school's orchestra played, imagining how she might conduct them one day.

After majoring in music in college, she felt ready to apply to some conducting training programs, but she wasn't accepted anywhere! So she began playing violin in various orchestras as a part-time freelancer and asked the conductors to give her private lessons in conducting. Sometimes the lessons involved just talk- ing about music, but one teacher would set up his apartment as if it were an orchestra. "The vacuum cleaner might be the violins," she recalls. "A plant was the woodwinds. We'd sing the music and I'd pretend to conduct." To get some *real* conducting experience, she started her own orchestra, made up of her friends. She conducted them so well that finally, at age 32, she won a spot in a summer conducting program where—surprise!—she studied with Leonard Bernstein. He became a fan, which helped her to at last land real conducting jobs. "Success means not giving up. If one avenue is closed to you, figure out another way to go."

Trail Blazers

Conductor Marin Alsop isn't the only musician featured in this book who did some trail blazing. Many of the others have also created their own special pathways, from Evelyn Glennie, who set out on her own as a pioneering solo percussionist, to Wynton Marsalis, who created a whole new organization—Jazz at Lincoln Center—to showcase jazz and educate thousands of kids and adults about this American art form. Pianist Wu Han and her husband started their own recording company—ArtistLed—because they grew frustrated dealing with regular recording companies.

A get-up-and-go attitude can help with another frustration: the fact that there are many more talented musicians than there are performing jobs. "The route a classical musician usually takes is to go to auditions, wait for opportunities to come to you," explains flutist Valerie Coleman. After earning a college degree in flute performance, she soon realized there are few openings each year in orchestra flute sections. Waiting for a job might take quite a while. "I didn't want to wait. I wanted to take matters into my own hands and create a career. In college, I hung out with jazz musicians and noticed that they form groups of their own, go out, and perform. Why doesn't this happen in classical music more?" Something else troubled this African American musician. "Growing up, I didn't have any African American classical-musician role models. It was a dream of mine to help young people, to be a role model for them." So in 1997 she started Imani Winds, a woodwind quintet made up of African American musicians.

This Grammy-nominated ensemble performs a range of music, from Maurice Ravel classics to pieces Ms. Coleman composes. At first, its members also did some freelancing, performing with other groups, to make ends meet. For several years, Jeff Scott, the group's horn player, was in the orchestra for the Broadway hit *The Lion King.* By the quintet's tenth year, however, it had so many concerts that its members didn't need to freelance much anymore. In addition to regular concerts, Imani Winds does hundreds of shows for kids. "Imani" is a word in the African language of Swahili that means "faith." As Ms. Coleman notes, you need "a lot of faith" to make it in music.

Spotlight On...

ANN HOBSON PILOT —Harp

Dream On: "I was about the only African American that I knew that played the harp from the time I started in high school until I got my first professional job," notes Ann Hobson Pilot, principal harpist with the Boston Symphony. "Someone said to me when I was about 15, 'If you want to play the harp, you're going to have to be twice as good as anybody else.' That could have been a discouraging thing to hear. But what I thought was, 'Well, I'll just have to work that hard.' Playing with an orchestra is something I had dreamed about since I first started on harp. I just kept going and never stopped." She points out that "in classical music, the competition is hard for anybody. But if you really want it and have talent and are willing to work hard, pursue your dreams. Sure, at times the problems got me down, but they didn't make me quit. I just worked harder."

Other Musical Doors

Sometimes, no matter how much people practice and love music they still may not become full-time performers. Some prefer a *non*-performing career in music, like Professor Michael Beckerman has. "In my late teens, I thought I was a fabulous pianist," he recalls. "Then I realized there were probably 500 other pianists in much better shape for making a career than I was. It doesn't have to do with how musical you are or if you practice. It's that everybody gets a gift and that wasn't mine. I didn't sit around crying about it. I was perfectly glad to do other things in music." He studied composing and musicology in college and is now head of the music department at New York University. Besides being a professor, he has also carved out an exciting extra career—giving pre-concert lectures at performances around the country and on television. He helps audiences get ready for the music they're about to hear so they can enjoy it more. "I also still play piano," he notes.

"I was perfectly glad to do other things in music."

Nancy Christensen, another would-be pianist, has also shifted to a non-performing career. "I always enjoyed the administrative side of music, even as a student," she observes. At the conservatory she attended after high school, she worked as an usher at the theater. After graduation, she got a job at Carnegie Hall in New York City, booking chamber ensembles to play recitals. Then she landed a job at Midori & Friends, a group that violinist Midori created to encourage musicians to visit schools to perform and teach. More recently, Ms. Christensen has been working for an agency that represents various musicians and ensembles, lining up performances for them around the country. She still makes time to practice piano because "it gives me such a feeling of joy. It lets me get out some of the frustrations of the day." For a while, she performed as the piano accompanist for friends' recitals. Now she has started giving private piano lessons to young children.

Other classmates of hers also have non-performing careers, working at recording companies or running music organizations. There are many other music-related careers, such as music librarian, lawyer for musicians, music reporter, music teacher, disk jockey, music-software developer, music store worker, music therapist (someone who uses music to help people with disabilities). The editors at Oxford University Press who helped bring this book to you are fine musicians: a flutist, organist, pianist, and a former opera singer, too. They use their music backgrounds to publish (and write) books on music. For more career ideas, talk with your teacher.

Spotlight On...

DAVID ROBINSON— Basketball, Piano, & Bass

In the Groove: "I started playing piano when I was 11," recalls basketball star David Robinson. "My dad played classical piano, and I loved listening to him. I had a lot of other stuff going on and didn't really practice. I started again after I got in the NBA, when I was about 25. That's when I started taking piano seriously. I also tried bass guitar. Bass is the instrument I enjoy most, although I spend more time on piano. Once I had a chance to go on stage to play bass with Harry Connick Jr.'s band. It was one of the scariest experiences of my life, and one of the most rewarding. I played the bass line to a song I knew that I'd played thousands of times in my room by myself. That made it a little easier. It was such a thrill to get in the groove with them. I like playing music because it's so deep. There's so much to it, so much to learn."

Money Makers

Some people started finding out what it's like to earn money from music when they were teenagers:

♦ **Gigs.** Susan landed a few jobs through her youth orchestra's assistant conductor, who often put together groups to play at various events and hired Susan when he needed an extra cellist. Other teens started their own groups. Rachel formed a quartet with other members of her youth orchestra. "The other kids got our first job playing at weddings," she explains. "People at the gig asked for our number so they could call us up to play for them. Our 'gig music' is mainly Baroque music which works well for most occasions." To set their fees, they asked around to find what other quartets in their area charge. Randy, a bass player who has performed with his own jazz and rock groups at weddings and parties, warns, "Have everything solid before a gig. If the band isn't grooving, you make yourself look bad."

♦ **Tutoring.** "My cello teacher suggested I do some teaching," says Susan, who tutored two younger kids who also took group lessons at school. "At first I was nervous," she says. "But once I started, I realized I had a lot I could teach them. The more I taught, the more I learned about cello. I finally realized what my teacher was telling me all these years was true—to play with a straight bow. I could never quite see what she meant. Watching my own students, I see it." To help guide teens in their tutoring, it's important for them to have a professional teacher to turn to for advice.

Spare Timers

Thousands of talented musicians have non-music jobs and play their instruments in their spare time, like Dr. Eugene Beresin, the piano-playing psychiatrist, and Dr. Yeou-Cheng Ma, the violin-playing pediatrician. Some have played non-stop since childhood. Others put their instruments on hold for a while, coming back to music later, which is what happened with Dr. Richard Clark. He was so busy during his medical training that he had no time to play cello anymore, an instrument he had loved playing ever since he was in sixth grade. But after completing his medical studies and settling in as a professor of radiology at the University of North Carolina, he has been playing up a storm, performing with a community orchestra and even organizing his own chamber music group that gives concerts at a local library. "I've met a whole different group of people through music, people I can talk about composers and music with instead of the last patient you had," he says. "My amateur musician friends are not nearly as uptight as some medical colleagues. Music is a freer and less stressful experience. Intellectually, it lets me use a different part of my brain."

There are even competitions just for amateurs, such as the IPCOA—the International Piano Competition for Outstanding Amateurs. Started in 1999, this competition's finalists have included lawyers, judges, doctors, architects, electrical engineers, stock market analysts, and business executives. There are even whole orchestras filled with spare-timers, such as the one Dr. Clark plays with in North Carolina. Boston has an orchestra made up mainly of health-care workers: the Longwood Symphony. It gives four concerts a year; money raised from ticket sales goes to charities that help the homeless or those with AIDS.

Musicians are tucked away in all sorts of professions, from James D. Wolfensohn, the cello-playing former head of the World Bank, to Barry Zito, the guitar-playing and Cy Young Award-winning pitcher for the San Francisco Giants. Here are a few others:

♦ **Robotics and Software Developer.** By day, Eric Rosenbaum is a graduate student at the Media Lab at MIT (Massachusetts Institute of Technology), helping to develop both a new computer language for kids and also robotics construction kits. But one night a month, he rehearses with a jazz band for people who used to go to Harvard, from which he graduated in 2001. When he was a student at Harvard, he played trombone in its jazz band, wind ensemble, and marching band. He also put together a funk band with friends. He kept up with the funk band for a while after college until his friends moved away. Now he plays mainly with the alumni jazz band. "It's cool to still get up and perform," he says. "Playing music has influenced me a lot. I'm thinking about creating new musical toys for kids."

♦ **Librarian.** While studying clarinet in high school, Georgiana McReynolds, a reference librarian at MIT, concentrated on solos and orchestral playing. "Now I prefer chamber music," she says. "With chamber music, you're more involved, even when you're not playing. You've got to really listen to what the other people are doing." She has played with chamber groups in the Boston area. For more than 10 years she has spent some of her vacation each summer attending a chamber music camp for adults. She likes the camp because of the new music she learns, the friends she makes, "and the fact that I can still play and get satisfaction out it."

♦ **Researcher.** Cancer researcher Dr. Bert Vogelstein, who has played piano since he was 11, formed a rock band with other scientists to play at scientific conventions they attend. "We practice one evening a week," says this doctor at Johns Hopkins Medical School in Baltimore. "Playing music transports me to a world filled with beautiful rhythm and sounds, free of the frustrations of research and ordinary life. It clears my mind so I can go back to the lab energized."

♦ **Designer.** Kitty Benton decided against a violin career when she was a student at the Juilliard School and realized she hated to perform. She became a designer of children's clothing instead, but plays in amateur string quartets as a hobby. "I won't perform," explains this New Yorker. "We play at someone's home just for fun."

On and On

That about wraps it up for this book's brainstorming session with our huge troupe of helpful pros and teens. But there's plenty more valuable advice waiting for you right in your own practice room at school, or in your teacher's studio, or at rehearsals for that ensemble you joined. If something's not quite working out for you musically, talk it over with other musicians or teachers. If they're like the ones interviewed for this book, they'll be glad you asked, and ready to give you an earful of savvy tips, to help you keep playing on and on.

"Play for the fun of it."

"Music can take you through all types of emotions: happy, sad, angry and everything else," notes Abby, a trombonist. "But I believe the most important thing about music is to enjoy it! Play for the fun of it."

Glossary

arpeggio Playing the notes of a chord separately, one after the other.

articulation The way in which notes are played, such as staccato or legato (*see below*).

audio interface A piece of equipment that permits sound recordings to be input into a computer.

chamber music Music for small groups of musicians in which each musician has a separate part to play.

chops Slang word for the abilities (physical and mental) needed to play an instrument.

concerto A piece of music in which a soloist plays with an orchestra; the plural is *concerti*.

dynamics How loudly or quietly notes are played.

embouchure The position lips need to be in to play a woodwind or brass instrument.

étude A piece of music designed to help a student practice certain technical skills; "study" in French.

fifth	In music, the interval between the first and fifth notes of a scale.
freelancer	Someone who works for various companies without being a permanent employee of them.
gig	Slang for a job playing music (pronounced with a hard "g" as in "good").
improvise	Making up music on the spur of the moment.
interval	The distance between two pitches.
intonation	How in tune a note is played.
legato	Playing a passage of notes very smoothly, with no pauses between the notes.
long tones	A warm-up for wind and brass instruments that involves playing a note a long time.
maestro	"Teacher" in Italian; a name often used for the conductor of an orchestra; the female form of the word is *maestra*.
metronome	A machine that clicks out the beat, which can be set at varying speeds.
MIDI file	A computer file that lets you hear a piece of music on a computer and also see the notes on the computer screen, if the computer has special music-notation software.
perfect fourth	In music, a fourth is the interval between the first and fourth notes of a scale; a perfect fourth is from C to F, or from G to C.
pitch	How high or low in tone a note is.
staccato	Playing a note for a very short time; a series of notes played this way will have brief silences between them; the opposite of legato.
tempo	The speed at which music is played.
woodshedding	Slang word for serious practicing.

Resource Guide

Suggestions for further reading, as well as information on some music-related organizations.

Books

Barber, David W. *Bach, Beethoven, and the Boys: Music History as It Ought to Be Taught*. Toronto, Canada: Sound and Vision, 1986.
A humorous (and sometimes zany) introduction to music history.

Beeching, Angela Myles. *Beyond Talent: Creating a Successful Career in Music*. New York: Oxford University Press, 2005.
Career advice for those thinking of becoming professional musicians.

Machover, Wilma, and Marienne Uszler. *Sound Choices: Guiding Your Child's Musical Experiences*. New York: Oxford University Press, 1996.
Written for parents, this book gives advice on all aspects of music instruction for kids. It has a huge resource guide, listing many organizations, books, and other materials that can help with everything from finding a teacher to coping with performance-related injuries.

Marsalis, Wynton. *Marsalis on Music*. New York: Norton, 1995.
This book by trumpeter Wynton Marsalis offers a lively introduction to music, with a helpful chapter on practicing. It's the companion book for a set of four videos for kids, also called *Marsalis on Music* (Sony), which features Mr. Marsalis, his jazz orchestra, Yo-Yo Ma, Seiji Ozawa, and the Tanglewood Music Center Orchestra.

Nathan, Amy. *Meet the Musicians: From Prodigy (or Not) to Pro*. New York: Henry Holt and Company, 2006.
This book introduces 15 New York Philharmonic musicians, telling how they got into music as kids and then describing the ups and downs they experienced on their way to landing at the Philharmonic.

Ristad, Eloise. *A Soprano on Her Head: Right-Side-Up Reflections on Life and Other Performances*. Moab, Utah: Real People Press, 1982.
This is not written for kids, but older students may enjoy taking a look at it for its wise and humorous advice on how to handle the jitters.

Westney, William. *The Perfect Wrong Note: Learning to Trust Your Musical Self*. Pompton Plains, New Jersey: Amadeus Press, 2006.
Advice from a music educator who feels that playing a wrong note doesn't have to be a total disaster, but can actually help you learn.

General Music Organizations

American Composers Forum
332 Minnesota Street, Suite East 145
St. Paul, MN 55101-1300
Telephone: 651-228-1407
Web site: www.composersforum.org/
The Web site for this group lists educational programs that can introduce kids to composing.

American Music Conference
5790 Armada Drive
Carlsbad, CA 92008-4391
Telephone: 760-431-9124
Web site: www.amc-music.com
This group's Web site gives news on how learning music can help students, and also has links to other music-related Web sites.

College Music Society
312 East Pine Street
Missoula, MT 59802

Telephone: 406-721-9616
Web site: www.music.org
Its Web site gives information
on colleges and universities that
offer music programs.

League of American Orchestras
33 West 60th Street
New York, NY 10023-7905
Telephone: 212-262-5161
Web site: www.american
orchestras.org
This group's Web site provides
a list of youth orchestras, as well
as links to Web sites of major
symphony orchestras.

**MENC: The National
Association for Music Education**
1806 Robert Fulton Drive
Reston, VA 22091
Telephone: 800-336-3768
Web site: www.menc.org
This group's Web site has
information on the educational
value of studying music.

**Music Teachers National
Association**
441 Vine Street, Suite 3100
Cincinnati, OH 45202-3004
Telephone: 513-421-1420
Web site: www.mtna.org
Its Web site lists certified music
teachers.

**National Academy of
Recording Arts & Sciences**
3402 Pico Boulevard

Santa Monica, CA 90405
Telephone: 310-392-3777
Web site: www.grammy.com
Here you can find information on
Grammy Award winners.

**National Guild of Community
Schools of the Arts**
520 Eighth Avenue, Suite 302
New York, NY 10018
Telephone: 212-268-3337
Web site: www.nationalguild.org/
This group's Web site lists music
schools and their Web sites.

Orchestras Canada
202-56 The Esplanade
Toronto ON M5E 1A7, Canada
Telephone: 416-366-8834
Web site: www.oc.ca
This group's site lists youth
orchestras in Canada and has
links for other Canadian music
organizations.

**Performing Arts Medicine
Association**
Web site: www.artsmed.org
This organization of physicians
and other professionals deals
with performing arts health
issues. Its site has links to
experts on performance-related
injuries.

**Suzuki Association
of the Americas**
P.O. Box 17310
Boulder, CO 80308

Telephone: 888-378-9854
Web site: http://suzukiassociation.org/
This site gives information about the Suzuki method and also lists Suzuki teachers.

VH1 Save The Music Foundation
1633 Broadway, 11th Floor
New York, NY 10019
Telephone: 212-654-7600
Web site: www.vh1.com/partners/save_the_music
This group sponsors musical instrument donation drives and other programs.

Web Sites of Instrument Organizations

Here are Web sites for organizations devoted to various instruments. To find other Web sites geared to your instrument, enter the name of your instrument at an Internet search engine.

American Harp Society
www.harpsociety.org

American Pianists Association
www.americanpianists.org

Guitar Foundation of America
www.guitarfoundation.org

International Clarinet Association
www.clarinet.org

International Double Reed Society
http://idrs.colorado.edu

International Horn Society
www.hornsociety.org

International Society of Bassists
www.isbworldoffice.com

International Trombone Association
www.ita-web.org

International Trumpet Guild
www.trumpetguild.org

International Women's Brass Conference
www.iwbc-online.org

Internet Cello Society
www.cello.org

National Flute Association, Inc.
www.nfaonline.org

North American Saxophone Alliance
www.saxalliance.org

Percussive Arts Society
www.pas.org

International Tuba Euphonium Association
www.iteaonline.org

Violin Society of America
www.vsa.to/

Other Web Sites

There are many other music Web sites. Here are a few that are fun to visit:

From the Top
www.fromthetop.com
This Web site for the public radio series (which features young performers) tells how to audition for the show.

Indiana University Cook Music Library
www.music.indiana.edu
This library site can be very helpful when doing musical research.

International Alliance for Women in Music
www.iawm.org
This has information on women performers and composers.

Science@NASA: Space Station Music
http://science.nasa.gov/headlines/y2003/04sep_music.htm
This Web page provides a link to a video of astronaut Ed Lu playing piano on board the International Space Station; there's also an article about other astronauts who have played instruments on NASA missions.

About the Troupe of Advisors

The Pros

A big round of applause goes to the professional musicians who found time in their busy schedules to be interviewed for this book. Here's more information on them, plus Web sites for those who have them.

John Adams, Pulitzer Prize-winning composer, has written orchestral works, such as the often-performed *Short Ride in a Fast Machine,* as well as several operas including *Nixon in China* and *Doctor Atomic.* In addition, he has served as a conductor with major orchestras in programs that combine his works with those of other composers. He grew up in New Hampshire and earned a bachelor and a master's degree in music from Harvard University. www.earbox.com

Marin Alsop in 2005 became the first woman to be named music director of a major U.S. orchestra, the Baltimore Symphony. She has been guest conductor for many other orchestras, as well as the Principal Conductor for Britain's Bournemouth Symphony and Music Director of the Colorado Symphony and the Cabrillo Festival of Contemporary Music. She grew up in New York City, attended Yale University, and earned degrees in violin performance from The Juilliard School. www.marinalsop.com

Joshua Bell started his violin career at age 14 when he won a *Seventeen* Magazine/General Motors competition and soloed with the Philadelphia Orchestra. He now gives more than 100 concerts a year and played the violin music for the movie "The Red Violin." He grew up in Indiana. www.joshuabell.com

David Bragunier, principal tuba player of the National Symphony from 1961 until retiring in 2004, has since been taking voice lessons and singing with the Washington Chorus. He grew up in Maryland and studied at Peabody Institute.

Barbara Butler, professor of trumpet at Northwestern University, plays with Chicago-based chamber music groups. She grew up in Iowa, and went to Northwestern University.

Valerie Coleman, flutist and founder of the woodwind quintet Imani Winds, is also a composer whose pieces are featured on the group's Grammy-nominated CD, "The Classical Underground." She grew up in Louisville, Kentucky, earned two bachelor's degrees—in flute performance and theory/composition—from Boston University, and a master's degree from Mannes College of Music. www.imaniwinds.com

Gustavo Dudamel was named Music Director of the Los Angeles Philharmonic in 2007 when he was just 26 years old. His tenure there starts in 2009. He had been Music Director for more than nine years of the Simón Bolívar Youth Orchestra of Venezuela, his native country. He has also served as guest conductor with major orchestras in Europe and the United States. www.gustavodudamel.com

James Galway performs worldwide, playing classical flute music as well as pop and Irish tunes. He grew up in Northern Ireland, studied at London's Royal College of Music, and was principal flutist with the Berlin Philharmonic. Sir James has won many prizes including being knighted in 2001 by Queen Elizabeth II of England. www.thegalwaynetwork.com

Evelyn Glennie performs as a solo percussionist around the world. She received a Grammy Award for one of her albums and has won many prizes, including the Order of the British Empire. She grew up in Scotland and attended the Royal Academy of Music in London. www.evelyn.co.uk

Hilary Hahn, a Grammy-winning violinist, began

studying violin in her hometown of Baltimore, Maryland. At age 10 she was admitted to Philadelphia's Curtis Institute of Music from which she graduated at age 19 with a bachelor's degree in music. She performs as a soloist around the world and also enjoys playing chamber music, reading, writing, bicycling, rowing, and learning languages.
www.hilaryhahn.com

Daniel Katzen, French horn player with the Boston Symphony, is on the faculty of the Boston University School for the Arts and New England Conservatory. He grew up in New York State, went to Indiana University School of Music, and did graduate studies at Northwestern.

Steven Mackey, Professor of Music at Princeton University, started out playing electric guitar in rock bands based in northern California, where he grew up. His interest shifted to classical music as an undergraduate at the University of California, Davis. He went on to earn advanced degrees in composition from Brandeis University and the State University of New York at Stony Brook. His compositions have won numerous awards and have been performed by major orchestras

and ensembles around the world.
www.stevenmackey.com

Wynton Marsalis, Artistic Director of Jazz at Lincoln Center, is a trumpeter (with Grammy Awards for jazz and classical albums), conductor, composer (winning the Pulitzer Prize in 1997), and music educator. He grew up in Louisiana, and attended Juilliard after high school.
www.wyntonmarsalis.org
www.jazzatlincolncenter.org

Peter Oundjian, Principal Conductor of the Caramoor Center for Music and Arts, was first violinist with the Tokyo String Quartet for many years. He grew up in England, and studied at the Royal College of Music and later at Juilliard.

Erika Nickrenz (piano), **Susie Park** (violin), and **Sara Sant'Ambrogio** (cello) are the members of the Eroica Trio, which has received Grammy nominations for its CDs and won first prize in 1991 in the Walter F. Naumburg Chamber Music Competition. In more than 80 concerts a year, the Trio plays new music as well as classics. Ms. Nickrenz, who grew up in New York, and Ms. Sant'Ambrogio, a Missouri native, are Juilliard graduates. Ms. Park grew up in Sydney,

Australia, and has a bachelor's degree from Curtis. www.eroicatrio.com

Adela Peña, a Juilliard graduate who grew up in New York City, performs with the Orpheus Chamber Orchestra and in various chamber groups and festivals since leaving the Eroica Trio, of which she was a founding member.

Ann Hobson Pilot, principal harpist with the Boston Symphony, helped found the Boston Music Education Collaborative, which brings music to kids in Boston public schools. She grew up in Pennsylvania, and studied at the Cleveland Institute of Music.

Joshua Redman, a Grammy-nominated jazz saxophonist who grew up in California, won first prize in the 1991 Theolonius Monk Institute of Jazz competition, shortly after graduating *summa cum laude* from Harvard. He tours extensively as the leader of his own ensembles and helped found the SFJazz Collective. www.joshuaredman.com

Paula Robison not only plays classical flute but also sizzling Brazilian choro music with her own choro band. A founding member of the Chamber Music Society of Lincoln Center, she grew up in California, attended Juilliard and soloed at age 20 with the New York Philharmonic. www.paularobison.com

Todd Seeber, double bass player with the Boston Symphony, was formerly principal bass with the Buffalo Philharmonic. He went to high school in Oregon, and attended Boston University.

Gil Shaham, Grammy Award–winning violinist, solos with orchestras around the world and has made several albums, including his hit, Vivaldi's "Four Seasons." As a young boy he lived in Israel, soloing with the Jerusalem Philharmonic at age 10. Then his family moved to New York. After high school, he enrolled in a joint program between Juilliard and Columbia University.

Susan Slaughter, principal trumpet player of the St. Louis Symphony, was the first woman to be principal trumpet of a major orchestra. She grew up in Indiana, and attended Indiana University.

Richard Stoltzman plays classical clarinet music, plus jazz, pop, and new music he has encouraged composers to write for clarinet.

This Grammy winner was the first wind player ever to win the Avery Fisher Prize. He grew up in California and Ohio, went to Ohio State University, and did graduate music studies at Yale.

Erica vonKleist plays saxophone with the Afro Latin Jazz Orchestra and has made recordings with many musicians, including Wynton Marsalis, as well as with her own quintet, Project E. She grew up in Connecticut, studied at the Manhattan School of Music and Juilliard, earning Juilliard's first-ever bachelor's degree in jazz. She has begun composing for jazz ensembles and directs the Afro-Latin Jazz Alliance Academy of Music, which teaches jazz in New York high schools. www.ericavonkleist.com

André Watts appeared on TV at age 16, soloing with the New York Philharmonic. Born in Germany (where his dad was in the U.S. Army), he moved to Pennsylvania at age eight. After high school, this pianist attended Peabody and now, in addition to performing with major orchestras around the world, he also teaches at Indiana University's Jacobs School of Music.

Wu Han, a pianist who grew up in Taiwan, appears regularly in prestigious venues across the United States, Europe, and the Far East as both a soloist and chamber musician. Her wide-ranging musical activities include the founding of ArtistLed, classical music's first musician-directed and Internet-based recording company. Wu Han and David Finckel serve as Artistic Directors of The Chamber Music Society of Lincoln Center and of the Music@ Menlo chamber music festival, which they founded in 2003. www.artistled.com

Teens and Teachers

Thanks also go to the more than 150 talented teens who share their tips in this book. They come from 22 states as well as from Canada, and filled out their questionnaires courtesy of the following schools and music programs: Boston University Tanglewood Institute; Carnegie Mellon University; D.C. Youth Orchestra; Eastman School of Music; Foxboro (Massachusetts) High School; Greater Dallas Youth Orchestra; Hartt School; Interlochen Arts Academy; Harlem School of the Arts; Hoff-Barthelson Music School; Indiana University; Juilliard School; Mamaroneck (New York) High School; New Bedford

(Massachusetts) Public Schools; North Carolina School of Music; Norwalk (Connecticut) Youth Symphony; Peabody Preparatory; Portland (Oregon) Youth Philharmonic; San Francisco Symphony Youth Orchestra; Wellesley (Massachusetts) Public Schools; Westerville (Ohio) South High School; West Hartford (Connecticut) Public Schools.

A big thank you also goes to the following teachers and administrators who arranged for teens to participate in this project and who, in a few cases, were interviewed themselves: Paul Barthelemy, Ruth Cahn, Tracey Elledge, Ann Farber, Byron Hanson, Karen Hill, Janet Kessin, Lunetta Knowlton, Shirley Leiphon, Steve Massey, Lyn McClain, Dr. Sandra Nicolucci, Natalie Ozeas, J. D. Parran, Ken Peck, Carolyn Phillips, Cynthia Plumb, Carole Prochazka, Carrie Root, John Salerno, Anita Schulz, Tom Serene, Haig Shahverdian, Catherine Sih, Howard Spindler, Maria Watkins, Jean Wynia, Michael Yaffe, Fran Zarubick. Other educators and performers who were interviewed and deserve a round of applause: Judah Adashi, Bina Breitner, Vanessa Breault Mulvey, Annette Costanzi, Mike Doll, Doreen Falby, Rebecca Henry, Dorothy DeLay, Polly Hunsberger, Dean Immel, Tom Jordan, Amy Rosen, Angela Taylor, and William Westney.

The 200 beginners who listed their musical gripes get a big thank you as well. They were students at: Fishkill (New York) Elementary School; Longy School of Music; Mohave Valley (Arizona) Junior High School; North Carolina School of the Arts; North Royalton (Ohio) Middle School; Rockland (Maine) Middle School; Saints Simon and Jude School (Louisville, Kentucky); Spokane (Washington) Public Schools; State College (Pennsylvania) Junior High School. Thanks also to their teachers: Bonnie Barry, Corine Cook, Pat French, Caroline McDowell, Michelle Nover, Marian Pedersen-Grover, Sharon Vardian, JoAnn Weatherbee, and Ross Wersonick.

Students in Photos Several schools and music programs helped provide photos of young musicians to serve as illustrations for this book, either by providing photos they already had in their files or by allowing photos to be taken specially for this book. A warm round of applause goes to:

- Boston University Tanglewood Institute (whose students are seen on pages 32, 48, 70)
- Children's Orchestra Society (page 147)
- Larchmont Music Academy (pages 9, 16, 26, 134, 141)
- Longy School of Music (page 5)
- The Juilliard School, Pre-College Division (pages 37, 54, 109)
- Mamaroneck High School (pages 2, 10, 20, 34, 50, 68, 90, 97, 106, 117, 132)
- St. Louis Symphony Orchestra's Youth Orchestra (pages 41, 62, 77, 121, 129, 144, 149, and the cover)

Other Supporters

The individuals listed here were also helpful in sharing their thoughts and providing encouragement for this project: Michael Asen, Elizabeth Baisley, Kitty Benton, Dr. Eugene Beresin, Aaron Bodling, Michael Beckerman, Carolann Buff, Dr. Christopher Carpenter, Nancy Christensen, Caleb Cochran, Colleen Conway, Donna Elaine, Ann Garside, Fred Geirsbach, John Goberman, Judy Gutmann, Mary Helton, Tim Hooker, Amy and Richard Hutchings, Adam Kent, Marigene Kettler, David Krenkel, Gary Larson, Julie Leenheer, Dr. Yeou-Cheng Ma, Dr. Ralph Manchester, Cathryn Mattson, Deborah Molodofsky, John Platoff, David Robinson, Rachelle Shollenberger, William Selden, Margaret Senko, Dora Shield, Joyce Slaubaugh, Nan Sommers, Genevieve Stewart, Lisa Stiller, Erica vanderLinde Feidner, Dr. Bert Vogelstein, Susan Whetle, Corey Widmer, librarians at the Larchmont Public Library, Ellen Clyne, Maribeth Anderson Payne, and Nancy Toff.

The following people were very helpful in putting together this new, updated edition of the book: Sarah Baird, Milina Barry, Shirley Bell, Rachel Benirschke, Katherine Benjamin, Darrin Britting, Mary Pat Buerkle, Jessica Chang, Dr. Richard Clark, Elena Cook,

Jane Covner, Charles Cumella, Dianne Darwin, Rebecca Davis, Tom Everett, Mary Lou Falcone, Mary Lou Francis, Heidi Frederick, Gayle G.Frere, Mike Gentry, Daniel Glen, Saskia Greenway, Norman Hirschy, Paul Hobson, Claudia and Steven Huter, Victoria Just, Dan Massoth, Georgiana McReynolds, Craig Monson, Peggy Neilson, Stephanie O'Neill, Michelle Pendoley, Leah Price, Julie Potter, Sue Rarus, Whitney E. Riepe, Eric Rosenbaum, Suzanne Ryan, Karen Stahl, Carol Stanton, Mary Ellen Stefanides, Adrienne Stortz, Svetlana Tsoneva, Lisa R. White, Leah Wilson-Velasco, John Yakubik, Matthew Zelle. Of course, special thanks go to my musical sons, Noah and Eric, and to my ever-enthusiastic and encouraging supporter (and fellow concert-goer), my husband, Carl.

Photo Credits

Cover, pp. 41, 62, 77, 121, 129, 144, 149—© Sarah Carmody; p. vi—© Charles J. Abbott (photograph appeared originally in *Reflections of Music* by Charles Abbott, published by Aspen Music Festival, 1987); pp. 2,10, 20, 34, 50, 68, 90, 97, 106, 132—© Richard Hutchings; p. 5—© 1998 Joshua Lavine; p. 6—courtesy of NASA; pp. 9, 16, 26, 47, 117, 122, 134, 141—© Amy Nathan; p. 12—© Michael Wilson; pp. 15, 85—© Christian Steiner, courtesy of Paula Robison and Wu Han; p. 18—© 1998 Chris Lee; p. 19—courtesy of Joshua and Shirley Bell;p. 23—© Mark Sink, courtesy of Joshua Bell; p. 24—© Glenn Ross; p. 27— photo by Nana Watanabe, © 1998 Sony Music, courtesy of Columbia Records; pp. 32, 48, 70—© Walter Scott, courtesy of Boston University Tanglewood Institute; pp. 37, 54, 109—© Nan Melville/iAfrikaPhotos; p. 38—© Boyd Hagen, courtesy of Deutsche Grammophon; p. 55—© Steve J. Sherman; p. 57—The Adrian Siegel Collection: The Philadelphia Orchestra Association Archives; p. 61—© Carol Weinberg, courtesy of Richard Stoltzman; p. 64—courtesy of Hilary Hahn; p. 74—© Paul Cox, courtesy of James Galway; pp. 42, 80, 86, 98—© Nina Choi; p. 83—courtesy of Jessica Chang; p. 92— courtesy of Wynton Marsalis; p. 94—© Robert Mottl, courtesy of Susan Slaughter; pp. 100, 101—© 2007 photo by Craig T. Mathew/Mathew Imaging; p. 104—© Charles J. Abbott;

p. 113—© Todd Gustafson;
p. 116—© Jeffrey Hornstein;
p. 119, 152—© Betsy Bassett, courtesy of Boston Symphony Orchestra; p. 126—© Sharon Ackerman Photography, courtesy of Joshua Redman;
p. 127—© William Haroutounian; p. 136—© Eric Nathan;
p. 138—© Michael Amsler;
p. 147—© Frank Gimpaya, courtesy of Yeou-Cheng Ma;
p. 150—© Grant Leighton;
p. 154—© 1999 Mark Langford, courtesy of David Robinson.

Text Credits

Excerpt on page 7 from *The Paula Robison Flute Warmups Book* © Copyright 1989 European American Music Corporation. All Rights Reserved. Used by permission of European American Music Corporation.

Excerpt on pages 35–6 from *Marsalis on Music* by Wynton Marsalis. Copyright © 1995 by Wynton Marsalis and Sony Classical USA. Reprinted by permission of W.W. Norton & Company, Inc.

Index